MONDAY   Patterning and Algebra

1. Colour the shapes to make a pattern. Circle the core of the pattern.

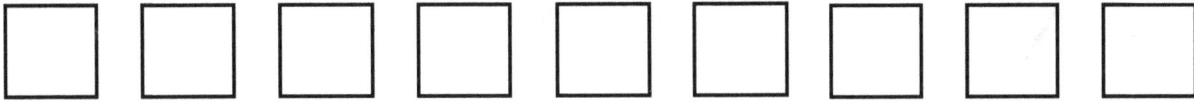

☐ ☐ ☐ ☐ ☐ ☐ ☐ ☐

What is your pattern rule? _____

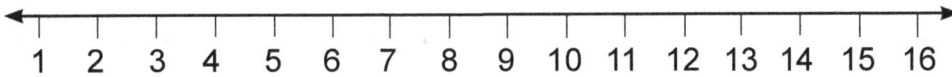

```
1  2  3  4  5  6  7  8  9  10 11 12 13 14 15 16
```

2. What is the missing number?

_____ + 8 = 12

3. Count on by 2s from 20.

20, _____, _____, _____

TUESDAY   Number Sense and Operations

1. What is the number?

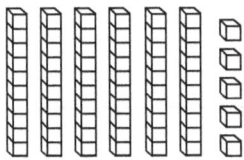

tens _____

ones _____

number _____

2. Write the numeral.

sixteen _____

3. Double the number then add one.

5 + 5 = _____

so 5 + 6 = _____

4. What is the name of this coin?

A. nickel

B. quarter

C. dime

WEDNESDAY Geometry

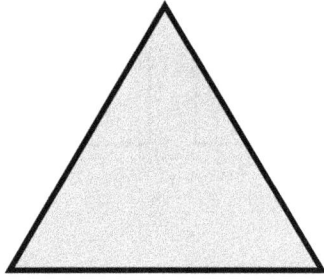

1. Circle the name of this shape.

   rectangle   triangle

2. How many sides does it have? _____

3. How many vertices does it have? _____

Trace and draw the shape.

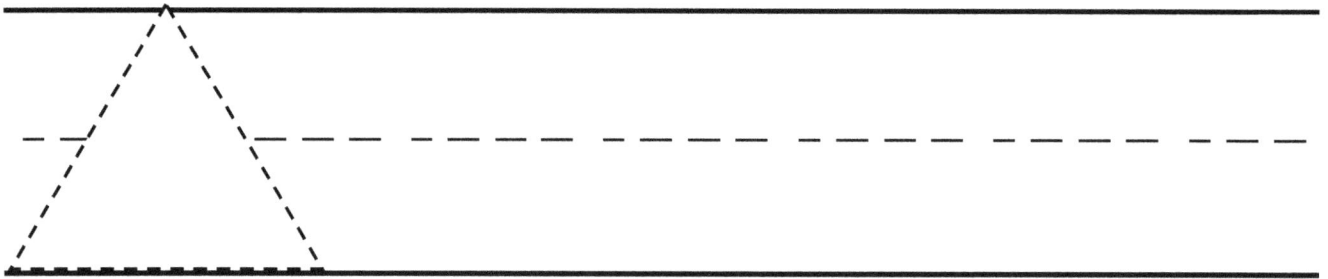

THURSDAY Measurement

1. What time is it?

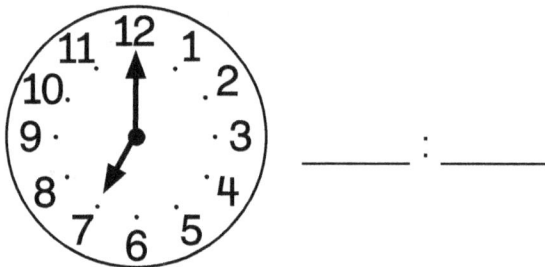

_____ : _____

2. Is the temperature hot or cold?

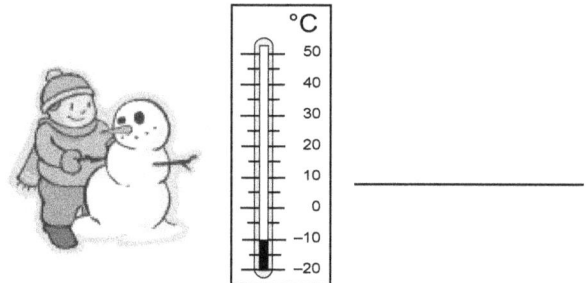

°C
50
40
30
20
10
0
−10
−20

_____

3. Which container holds more?

A.   B.

4. Measure the length of the line.

It is about _____ 👟 long.

Mr. Tate's students conducted a survey of their favourite pets.
Use the pictograph to answer the questions about the results.

Favourite Pets

Dog		
Bird		
Cat		

1. How many students chose 🐕 ? _____

2. How many students chose 🐱 ? _____

3. Circle the pet students chose the most.

4. Circle the pet students chose the least.

BRAIN STRETCH

The clown had 5 red balloons and 4 blue balloons.
How many balloons did the clown have in all?

MONDAY — Patterning and Algebra

1. Colour the shapes to make a pattern. Circle the core of the pattern.

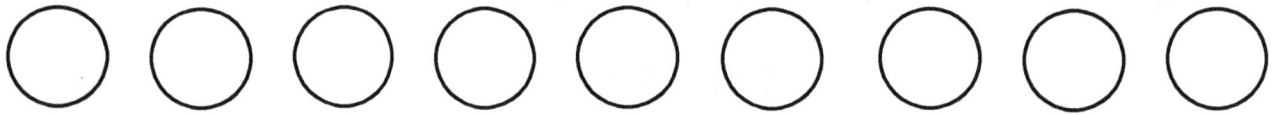

◯ ◯ ◯ ◯ ◯ ◯ ◯ ◯ ◯

What is your pattern rule? _____

2. What is the missing number?

_____ + 4 = 10

3. Count on by 10s from 70.

70, _____, _____, _____

TUESDAY — Number Sense and Operations

1. What is the number?

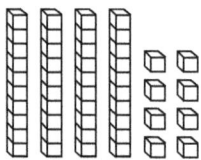

tens _____

ones _____

number _____

2. Write the numeral.

A. ten _____

B. thirteen _____

3. Double the number then add one.

4 + 4 = _____

so 4 + 5 = _____

4. What is the name of this coin?

A. nickel
B. quarter
C. loonie

WEDNESDAY Geometry

1. Circle the name of this shape.

        circle   triangle

2. How many sides does it have? _____

3. How many vertices does it have? _____

Trace and draw the shape.

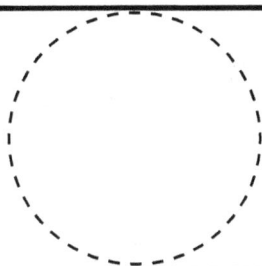

THURSDAY Measurement

1. Which tool would be best to measure the length of a book?

    A. scale

    B. measuring tape

    C. clock

2. Choose the better unit of measure for the weight of a cat.

    A. gram

    B. kilogram

3. Which container holds less?

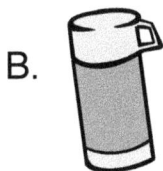

A.   B.

4. Measure the length of the line.

It is about _____ long.

Ms. Richardson's students conducted a survey of their favourite ice cream flavours. Use the pictograph to answer the questions about the results.

Favourite Ice Cream Flavour

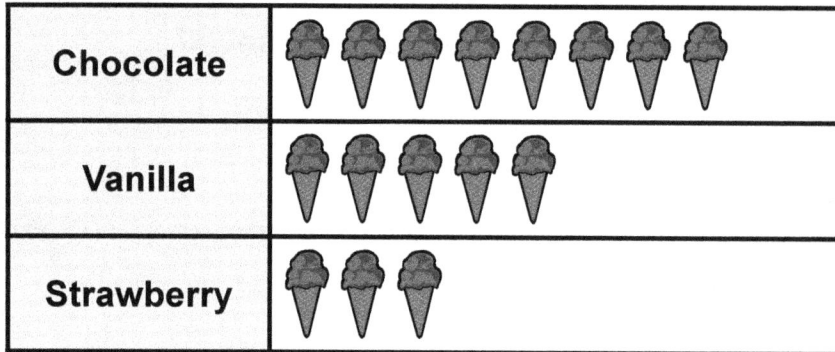

Chocolate	🍦🍦🍦🍦🍦🍦🍦🍦
Vanilla	🍦🍦🍦🍦🍦
Strawberry	🍦🍦🍦

One 🍦 stands for 1 vote.

1. How many students liked chocolate? _____

2. How many students liked vanilla? _____

3. How many students liked strawberry? _____

4. How many students voted? _____

BRAIN STRETCH

There were 15 ants on a log. 9 ants walked away. How many ants were left?

MONDAY — Patterning and Algebra

1. Colour the shapes to make a pattern. Circle the core of the pattern.

⬡ ⬡ ⬡ ⬡ ⬡ ⬡ ⬡ ⬡ ⬡

2. Meg was adding 7 + 5 + 3.
   I know that 7 + 3 = 10 and
   then I can add 5 more.
   The answer is 10 + 5 = 15.

   Try your own way to add 6 + 8 + 4.

   _____

TUESDAY — Number Sense and Operations

1. What is the number?

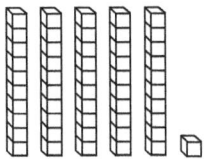

   tens _____
   ones _____
   number _____

2. A. 74 = _____ tens

   _____ ones

   B. 82 = _____ tens

   _____ ones

4. What is the name of this coin?

   A. nickel
   B. quarter
   C. loonie

3. Circle the third turtle.

WEDNESDAY Geometry

1. Circle the name of this shape.

square   triangle

2. How many sides does it have? _____

3. How many vertices does it have? _____

Trace and draw the shape.

THURSDAY Measurement

1. What time is it?

_____ : _____

2. Estimate how long it would take to sneeze.

A. less than one minute
B. more than one minute

3. When do most people have their bedtime?

A. a.m.
B. p.m.

4. Measure the length of the line.

It is about _____ 👟 long.

Data Management

Here are the results of a Favourite Shape Survey.
Use the data from the pictograph to make a bar graph. Answer the questions.

Favourite Shape

Circle	◯ ◯ ◯ ◯ ◯ ◯
Triangle	△ △ △ △
Square	▢ ▢
Rectangle	▯ ▯ ▯ ▯

1. How many people answered the survey? _____

2. What was the most popular shape? _____

3. What was the least popular shape? _____

4. Which shapes have the same number of votes? _____

BRAIN STRETCH

Carolyn had 18 pieces of bubble gum. She gave 9 pieces to Mike.
How many pieces of bubble gum did she have left?

MONDAY — Patterning and Algebra

1. Count by 2s on the chart. Colour the numbers.

   What patterns do you see?

   _____

   _____

2. What is the missing number in the sequence?

   64, 66, 68, _____, 72, 74,

1	2	3	4	5	6	7	8	9	10
11	12	13	14	15	16	17	18	19	20
21	22	23	24	25	26	27	28	29	30
31	32	33	34	35	36	37	38	39	40
41	42	43	44	45	46	47	48	49	50
51	52	53	54	55	56	57	58	59	60
61	62	63	64	65	66	67	68	69	70
71	72	73	74	75	76	77	78	79	80
81	82	83	84	85	86	87	88	89	90
91	92	93	94	95	96	97	98	99	100

TUESDAY — Number Sense and Operations

1. What is the number?

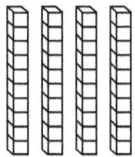

   tens _____

   ones _____

   number _____

2. Compare the numbers. Use <, >, or =.

   A. 58 ☐ 56

   B. 99 ☐ 99

3. Circle the first hippopotamus.

4. What is the name of this coin?

   A. nickel
   B. dime
   C. quarter

WEDNESDAY Geometry

1. Circle the name of this shape.

    rectangle   triangle

2. How many sides does it have? _____

3. How many vertices does it have? _____

Trace and draw the shape.

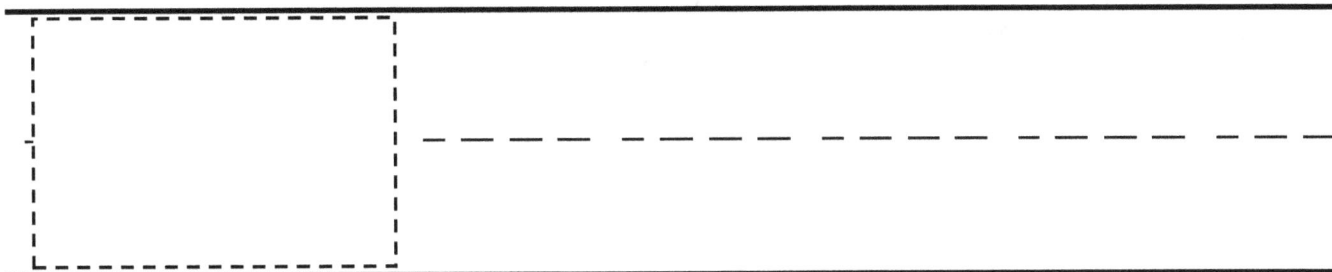

THURSDAY Measurement

1. What time is it?

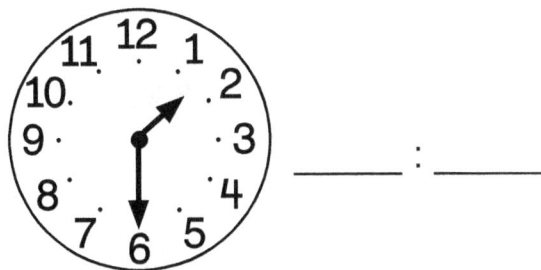

_____ : _____

2. Circle the container that holds more.

A. 1 Litre   B. 4.5 Litres

3. Which is a better estimate for the height of a tree?

A. 20 metres tall

B. 20 centimetres tall

4. Measure the length of the line.

It is about _____ 👟 long.

Ms. Turnbull's class conducted a survey about favourite kinds of cake. Use the pictograph to answer the questions about the results.

Favourite Cake

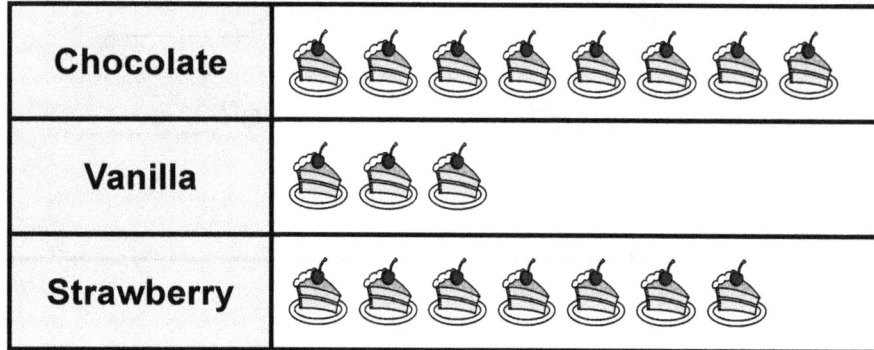

Chocolate	🍰🍰🍰🍰🍰🍰🍰🍰
Vanilla	🍰🍰🍰
Strawberry	🍰🍰🍰🍰🍰🍰🍰

Each piece of 🍰 stands for 1 vote.

1. How many students liked chocolate? _____

2. How many students liked vanilla? _____

3. How many students liked strawberry? _____

4. How many students voted? _____

BRAIN STRETCH

Howard had 22 stamps. He got 10 more.
How many stamps does Howard have in all?

MONDAY Patterning and Algebra

1. Count by 5s on the chart. Colour the numbers.

   What patterns do you see?

   _____

   _____

2. What is the missing number in the sequence?

   70, 75, 80, _____, 90, 95

1	2	3	4	5	6	7	8	9	10
11	12	13	14	15	16	17	18	19	20
21	22	23	24	25	26	27	28	29	30
31	32	33	34	35	36	37	38	39	40
41	42	43	44	45	46	47	48	49	50
51	52	53	54	55	56	57	58	59	60
61	62	63	64	65	66	67	68	69	70
71	72	73	74	75	76	77	78	79	80
81	82	83	84	85	86	87	88	89	90
91	92	93	94	95	96	97	98	99	100

TUESDAY Number Sense and Operations

1. What is the number?

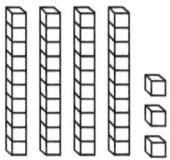

   tens _____

   ones _____

   number _____

2. Circle the fourth robot.

3. Order the numbers from least to greatest.

   74, 46, 20

   _____ < _____ < _____

4. Write the number.

   A. 10 more than 5 _____

   B. 10 less than 20 _____

WEDNESDAY Geometry

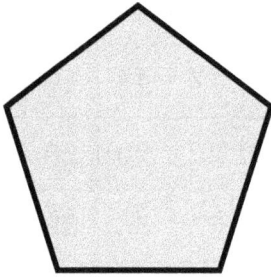

1. Circle the name of this shape.

   rectangle   pentagon

2. How many sides does it have? _____

3. How many vertices does it have? _____

Trace and draw the shape.

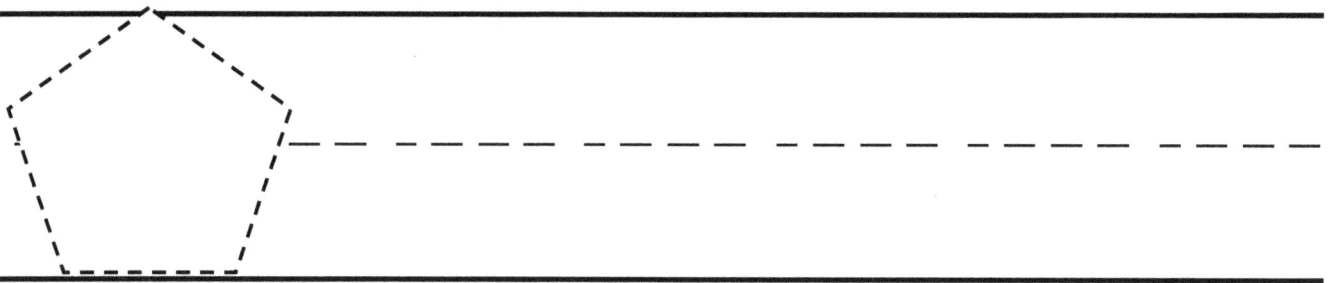

THURSDAY Measurement

1. What time is it?

   _____ : _____

2. What month comes after November?

   _____

3. Which tool would be best to tell when it is time for recess?

   A. scale
   B. calendar
   C. clock

4. Measure the length of the line.

   It is about _____ 👟 long.

Week 5

Ms. Smith's class took a survey of favourite sports.
Use the pictograph to answer the questions about the results.

Favourite Sport

Soccer	☺ ☺ ☺ ☺
Basketball	☺ ☺ ☺ ☺ ☺ ☺ ☺ ☺
Hockey	☺ ☺ ☺ ☺ ☺

Each ☺ stands for 2 votes.

1. How many students liked soccer? _____

2. How many students liked basketball? _____

3. How many students liked hockey? _____

4. How many more students liked basketball more than hockey? _____

BRAIN STRETCH

Santos had 13 apples. He needed 20 apples to bake some apple pies.
How many more apples does Santos need?

MONDAY — Patterning and Algebra

1. Count by 10s on the chart. Colour the numbers.

What patterns do you see?

_____

_____

2. What is the missing number in the sequence?

40, 50, 60, _____, 80, 90

1	2	3	4	5	6	7	8	9	10
11	12	13	14	15	16	17	18	19	20
21	22	23	24	25	26	27	28	29	30
31	32	33	34	35	36	37	38	39	40
41	42	43	44	45	46	47	48	49	50
51	52	53	54	55	56	57	58	59	60
61	62	63	64	65	66	67	68	69	70
71	72	73	74	75	76	77	78	79	80
81	82	83	84	85	86	87	88	89	90
91	92	93	94	95	96	97	98	99	100

TUESDAY — Number Sense and Operations

1. What is the number?

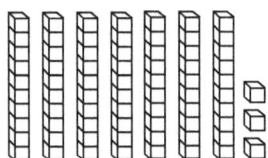

tens _____
ones _____
number _____

2. Write the number.

A. 10 more than 8 _____

B. 5 less than 21 _____

3. A. 57 = _____ tens
_____ ones

B. 82 = _____ tens
_____ ones

4. What is the name of this coin?

A. quarter _____

B. toonie _____

C. nickel _____

WEDNESDAY   Geometry

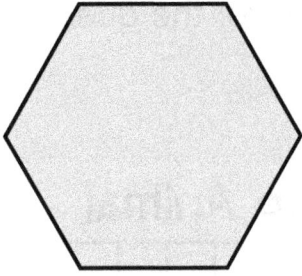

1. Circle the name of this shape.

   rectangle   hexagon

2. How many sides does it have? _____

3. How many vertices does it have? _____

Trace and draw the shape.

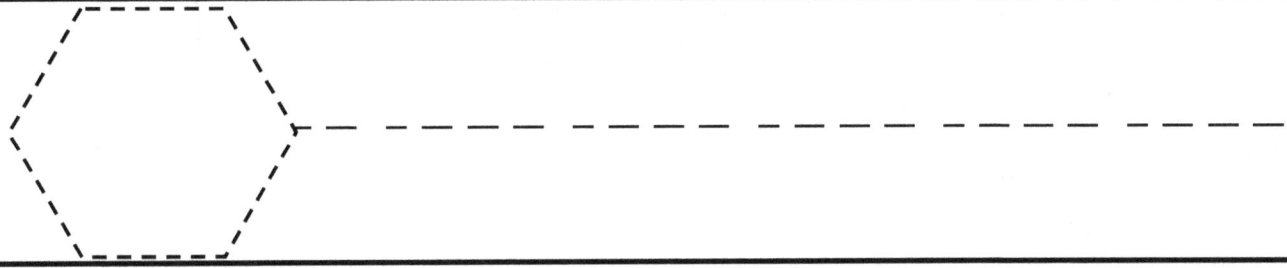

THURSDAY   Measurement

1. Which tool would be best to measure the weight of a bag of apples?

   A. scale

   B. ruler

   C. measuring cup

2. What is the better estimate of the length of a car?

   A. more than 1 metre

   B. less than 1 metre

3. Is the temperature hot or cold?

   A. hot

   B. cold

4. Measure the length of the line.

   It is about _____ 👟 long.

Here are the results of a Favourite Zoo Animal Survey.
Use the data from the pictograph to make a bar graph. Answer the questions.

Favourite Zoo Animal

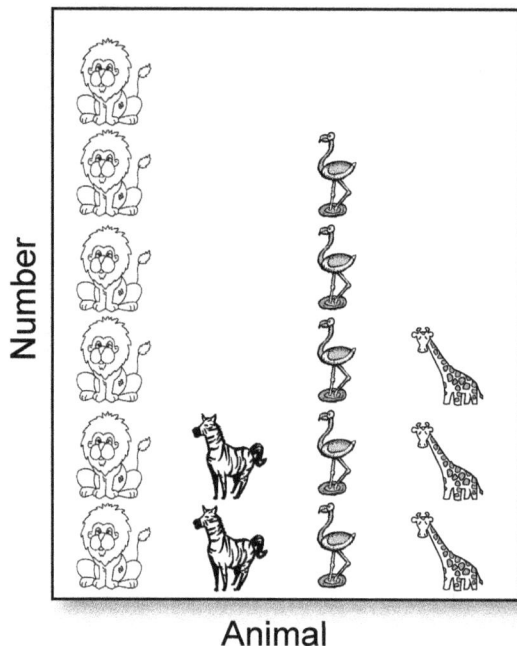

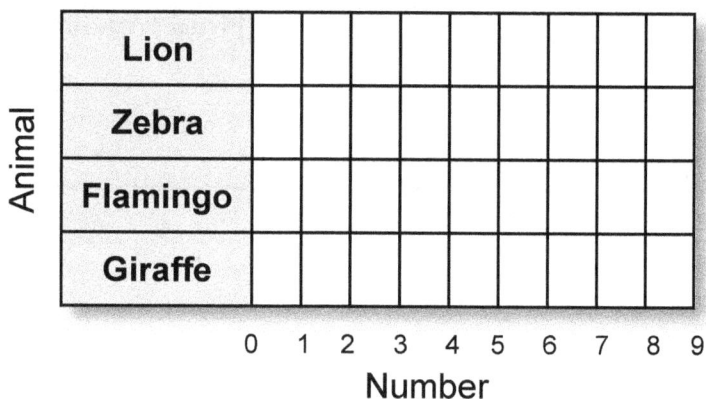

Number

Animal

Favourite Zoo Animal

Animal										
Lion										
Zebra										
Flamingo										
Giraffe										

0 1 2 3 4 5 6 7 8 9

Number

1. How many people answered the survey? _____

2. What was the most popular zoo animal? _____

3. What was the least popular zoo animal? _____

4. How many voted for either a lion or zebra? _____

BRAIN STRETCH

George had 15 stamps. Carlos had 22 stamps.
How many more stamps did Carlos have?

MONDAY · Patterning and Algebra

1. Extend the number pattern.

   3, 6, 9, _____, _____, _____

3. What is the missing number?

   _____ − 5 = 8

2. There are 7 goldfish in the tank. Maria got 6 more goldfish. How many goldfish are in the tank now? Use pictures and an equation to show your work.

   7 + 6 = [ ]

   _____ goldfish

4. Extend the pattern. Circle the core of the pattern.

   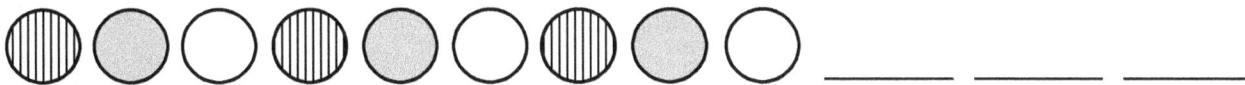 _____ _____ _____

   What is your pattern rule? _____

TUESDAY · Number Sense and Operations

1. What is the number?

   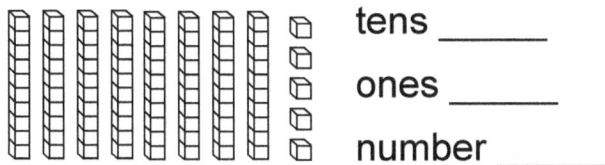 tens _____
   ones _____
   number _____

2. Write = or ≠ to make the number sentence true.

   15 − 9 [ ] 5 + 4

3. Double the number and subtract one.

   8 + 8 = _____

   so 8 + 7 = _____

4. What is the value of the coins?

    _____ ¢

WEDNESDAY Geometry

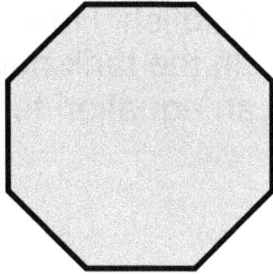

1. Circle the name of this shape.

   triangle   octagon

2. How many sides does it have? _____

3. How many vertices does it have? _____

Trace and draw the shape.

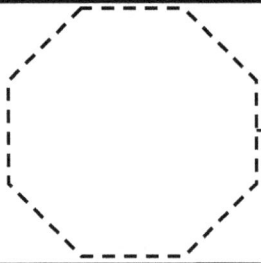

THURSDAY Measurement

1. Draw in the hands on the clock to show the time 5:00.

2. Andrew went to the park from 1:00 to 3:00. How long was he at the park?

   _____ hours

3. Draw a line 2 centimetres long.

4. Measure the length of the line.

   It is about _____ 👟 long.

FRIDAY Data Management

Ms. Lopez's class conducted a survey of their favourite fruits.
Use the pictograph to answer the questions about the results.

Favourite Fruit

Orange	◯ ◯ ◯ ◯ ◯ ◯ ◯
Apple	🍎 🍎 🍎 🍎
Watermelon	🍉 🍉 🍉 🍉 🍉 🍉

1. How many students liked ◯ ? _____

2. How many students liked 🍎 ? _____

3. How many students liked 🍉 ? _____

4. How many students voted? _____

5. Which fruit was the most popular? _____

BRAIN STRETCH

There are 9 blue pens and 5 green pens on the table. Tom put 3 more pens on the table. How many pens are there now? Use pictures and the equation to show your work.

9 + 5 + 3 = ☐

_____ pens

MONDAY — Patterning and Algebra

1. Count on by 5s from 100.

   100, _____, _____, _____, _____

2. What is the missing number?

   _____ + 7 = 14

3. Extend the pattern. Circle the core of the pattern.

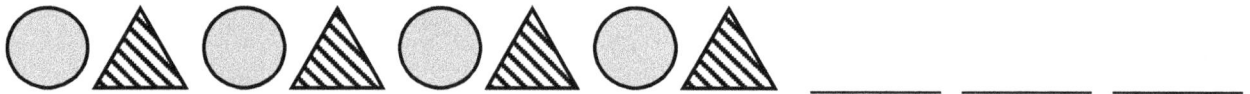

   ○ ▲ ○ ▲ ○ ▲ ○ ▲ ○ ▲ _____ _____ _____

   What is your pattern rule? _____

TUESDAY — Number Sense and Operations

1. What is the number?

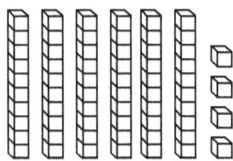

   tens _____
   ones _____
   number _____

2. Write = or ≠ to make the number sentence true.

   18 – 10 [   ] 11 + 1

3. What number comes just before?

   A. _____, 81

   B. _____, 36

4. What is the value of the coins?

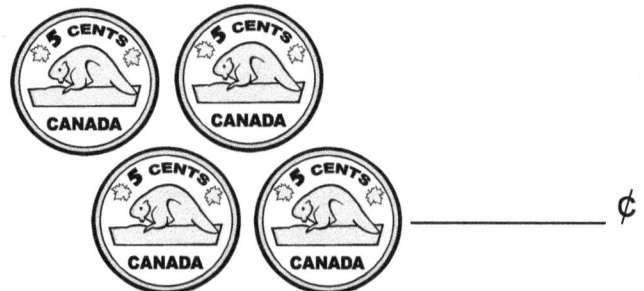

   _____ ¢

WEDNESDAY Geometry

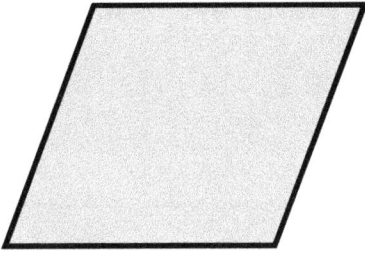

1. Circle the name of this shape.

   parallelogram   circle

2. How many sides does it have? _____

3. How many vertices does it have? _____

Trace and draw the shape.

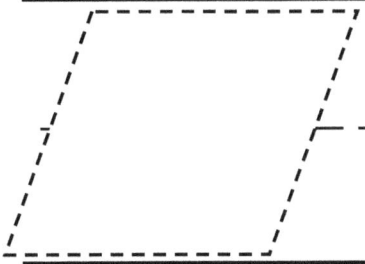

THURSDAY Measurement

1. What time is it?

_____ : _____

2. Dave left the house at 3:30 and came back at 7:30. How long was he gone?

   _____ hours

3. What day of the week comes after Monday?

   A. Tuesday
   B. Friday
   C. Sunday

4. Draw a line 3 centimetres long.

Here are the results of a Pet Survey.
Complete the chart and bar graph. Answer the questions about the results.

Favourite Pets Chart

Pet	Tally	Number
Dog		9
Cat		7
Hamster		4
Bird		2

Favourite Pets Graph

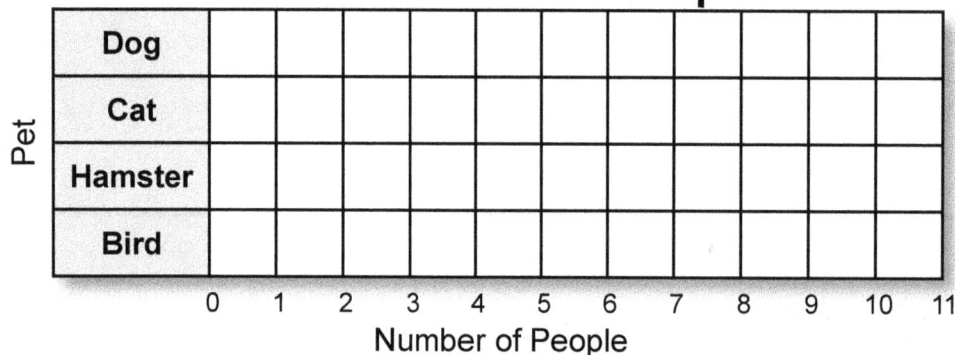

Pet											
Dog											
Cat											
Hamster											
Bird											

0 1 2 3 4 5 6 7 8 9 10 11
Number of People

1. What was the most popular pet? _____

2. What was the least popular pet? _____

3. How many people chose either a dog or a bird? _____

4. How many more people chose a cat than a hamster? _____

BRAIN STRETCH

1.
```
   3
   8
+ 2
```

2.
```
   7
   6
+ 7
```

3.
```
  11
-  5
```

4.
```
  18
-  9
```

MONDAY Patterning and Algebra

1. What is the missing number in this number pattern?

    55, _____, 75, 85, 95

2. Pat was subtracting 15 − 9.
   I know 9 + 6 = 15
   so 15 − 9 = 6.

    Try Pat's way to solve 13 − 8.

3. Extend the pattern. Circle the core of the pattern.

   ■ □ ■ □ ■ _____ _____

   What is your pattern rule? _____

TUESDAY Number Sense and Operations

1. What is the number?

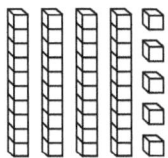

   tens _____
   ones _____
   number _____

2. Compare the numbers. Use <, >, or =.

   78 [   ] 87

3. Double the number, then subtract 1.

   9 + 9 = _____

   so 9 + 8 = _____

4. What is the value of the coins?

   _____ ¢

WEDNESDAY Geometry

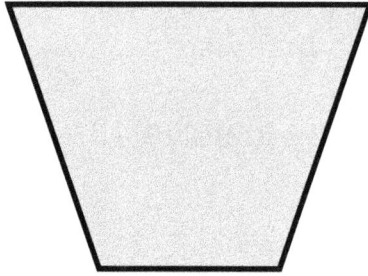

1. Circle the name of this shape.

   trapezoid   circle

2. How many sides does it have? _____

3. How many vertices does it have? _____

Trace and draw the shape.

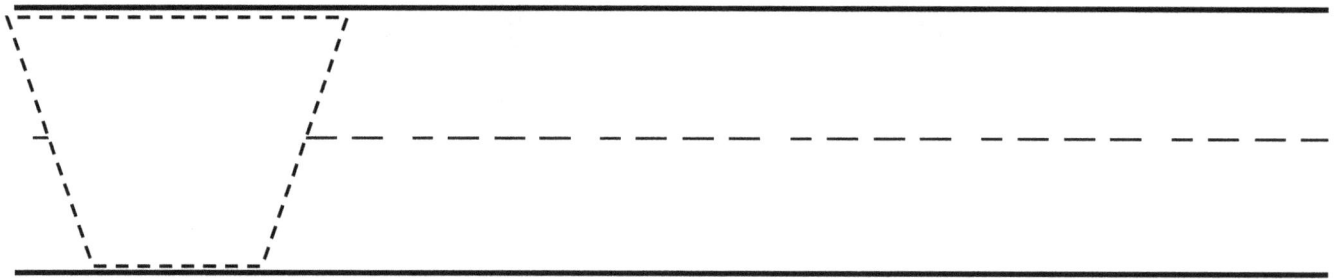

THURSDAY Measurement

1. What time is it?

   _____ : _____

2. When do you leave for school in the morning?

   A.   a.m.

   B.   p.m.

3. What day of the week is between Thursday and Saturday?

   _____

4. Which tool would be best to measure the temperature?

   A.   scale

   B.   thermometer

   C.   clock

Here are the results of a Favourite Cookie Survey. Complete the chart.
Answer the questions about the results.

Favourite Cookie Graph

Chocolate Chip	🍪 🍪 🍪 🍪 🍪 🍪
Oatmeal Raisin	🍪 🍪 🍪 🍪
Gingerbread	🍪 🍪

Each 🍪 stands for 2 votes.

Favourite Cookie Chart

Cookie	Tally	Number
Chocolate Chip		
Oatmeal Raisin		
Gingerbread		

1. How many students liked chocolate chip? _____

2. How many students liked oatmeal raisin? _____

3. How many more students chose chocolate chip than gingerbread? _____

4. Which cookie did students like the most? _____

BRAIN STRETCH

1.	2.	3.	4.
22 + 3	36 − 2	40 + 3	28 − 2

MONDAY — Patterning and Algebra

1. What is the missing number in this number pattern?

   32, 42, _____, 62, 72

   Pattern rule _____

2. What is the missing number?

   _____ + 4 = 10

3. Create a pattern where only the size of the shape changes. Circle the core of the pattern.

   _____

TUESDAY — Number Sense and Operations

1. What is the number?

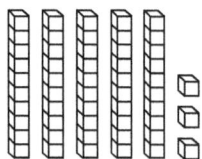

   tens _____
   ones _____
   number _____

2. What are two related facts for 8 + 2 = 10?

   _____ + _____ = _____

   _____ − _____ = _____

3. Complete the equations. Use only tens and ones.

   A. 84 = _____ + _____

   B. 29 = _____ + _____

4. What is the value of the coins?

   _____ ¢

WEDNESDAY Geometry

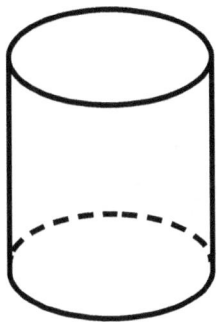

1. Circle the name of this 3D shape.

cylinder   pyramid

2. How many edges does it have? _____

3. How many faces does it have? _____

4. Look at the shapes. Choose flip, slide, or turn.

♡ → ♡

A. flip
B. slide
C. turn

THURSDAY Measurement

1. What time is it?

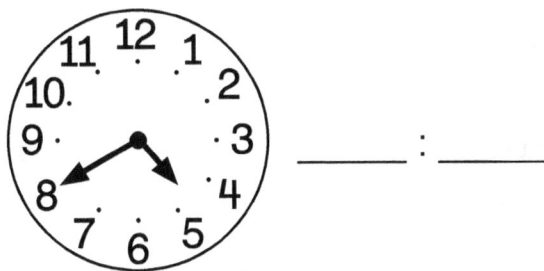

_____ : _____

2. What time will it be in 4 hours?

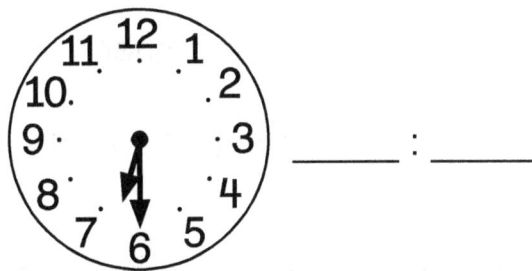

_____ : _____

3. How many months in a year?

_____ months

4. Which tool would be best to measure the width of a window?

A. scale
B. metre stick
C. clock

Count the pictures and complete the favourite shape bar graph. Answer the questions.

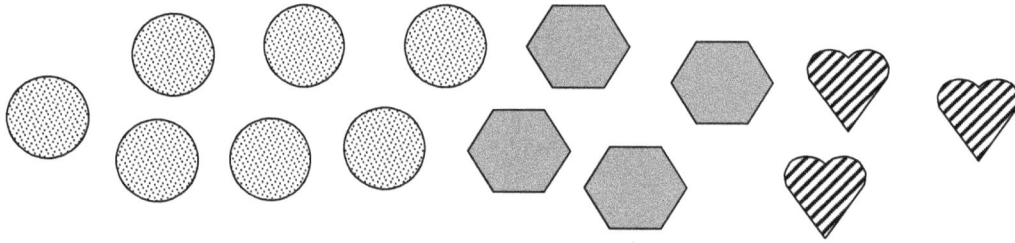

Favourite Shape Graph

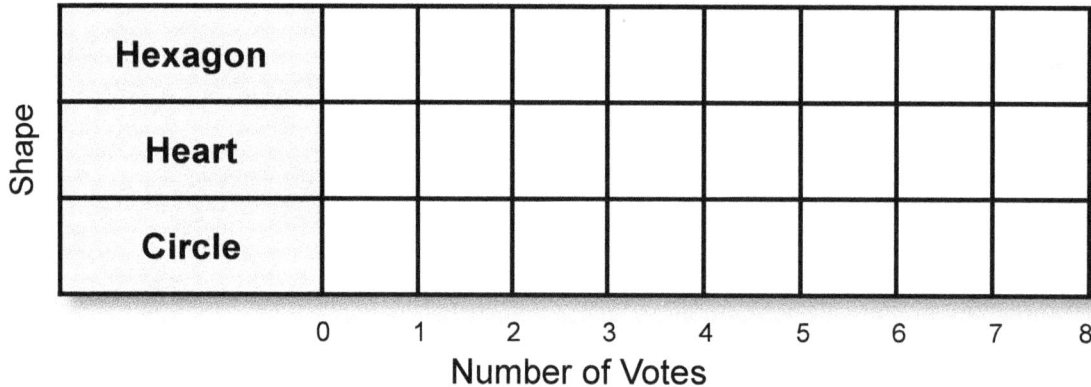

Shape									
Hexagon									
Heart									
Circle									

0 1 2 3 4 5 6 7 8
Number of Votes

1. Which shape is the most popular? _____

2. Which shape is the least popular? _____

3. How many votes altogether? _____

4. How many more votes for circle than heart? _____

BRAIN STRETCH

1.
```
  15
+  2
____
```

2.
```
  20
−  6
____
```

3.
```
  23
+  4
____
```

4.
```
  38
−  3
____
```

MONDAY Patterning and Algebra

1. What is the missing number?

   _____ + 5 = 11

2. There are 4 balls in a box. Jill put some more balls in the box. There are now 13 balls in the box. How many balls did Jill put in? Use pictures and the equation to show your work.

   4 + ☐ = 13

   _____ balls

3. Extend the pattern.

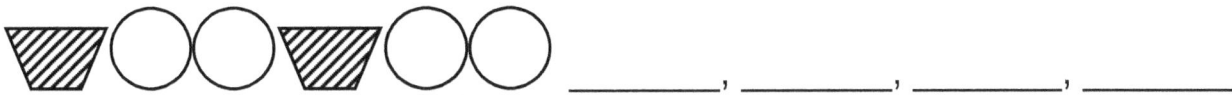

   ▽ ◯ ◯ ▽ ◯ ◯ ◯ _____, _____, _____, _____

   What is the pattern rule? _____

TUESDAY Number Sense and Operations

1. What is the number?

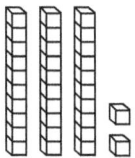

   tens _____
   ones _____
   number _____

2. Pair the circles. Are any circles left over? _____

   Is the number 4 odd or even? _____

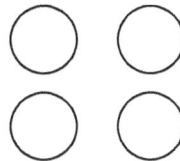

   ◯ ◯
   ◯ ◯

3. Colour to show $\frac{3}{4}$.

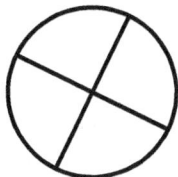

4. What is the value of the coins?

   _____ ¢

© Chalkboard Publishing

WEDNESDAY — Geometry

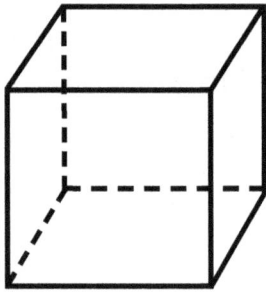

1. Circle the name of this 3D shape.

    cube   pyramid

2. How many edges does it have? _____

3. How many faces does it have? _____

4. Draw a circle.

5. What a shape is inside the square?

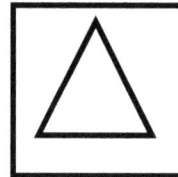

    A. triangle
    B. square

THURSDAY — Measurement

1. What time is it?

    half past _____

2. What day of the week comes just before Wednesday?

    A. Tuesday
    B. Friday
    C. Monday

3. When do most people eat dinner?

    A. a.m.
    B. p.m.

4. What is a better estimate for the length of a classroom?

    A. 30 metres
    B. 30 centimetres

Week 11

Here are the results of a favourite vegetable survey.
Use the data from the bar graph to answer the questions.

Favourite Vegetable

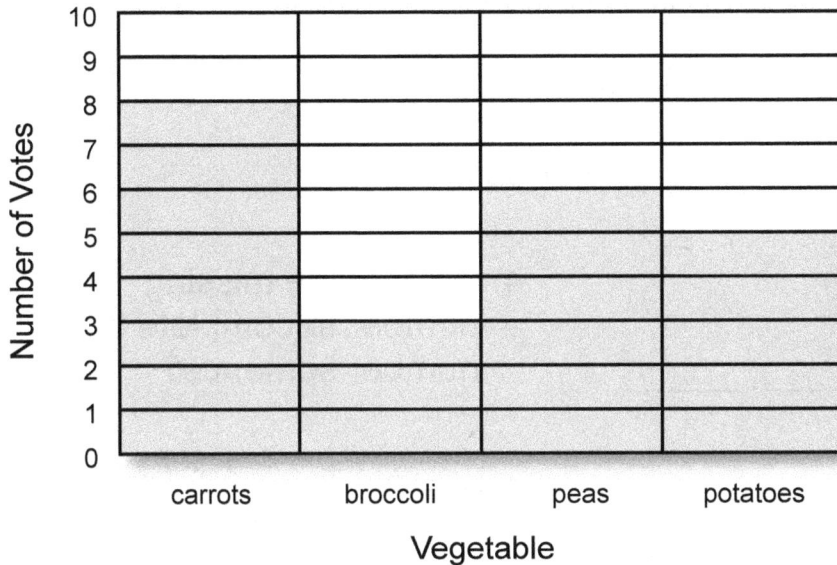

1. Which vegetable has the least votes? _____

2. How many more votes are there for carrots than broccoli? _____

3. Which vegetable is the most popular? _____

4. How many votes for peas and potatoes combined? _____

BRAIN STRETCH

1.
```
  74
+ 15
____
```

2.
```
  31
+ 20
____
```

3.
```
  98
- 68
____
```

4.
```
  87
- 55
____
```

MONDAY — Patterning and Algebra

1. What is the missing number?

    _____ + 8 = 11

2. There are 7 soccer balls in the gym. Lewis took 4 balls outside. Clark put 8 more soccer balls in the gym. How many soccer balls are in the gym now? Use pictures and the equation to show your work.

    7 – 4 + 8 = ☐

    _____ soccer balls

3. Count on by 10s from 120.

    120, _____, _____, _____, _____

4. What is the missing number to complete the number sentence?

    _____ + 9 = 2 + 7

TUESDAY — Number Sense and Operations

1. What is the number?

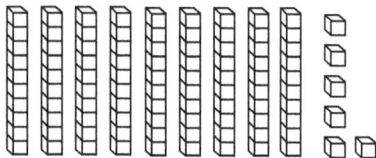

    tens _____
    ones _____
    number _____

2. Compare the numbers. Use <, >, or =.

    41 ☐ 35

3. Write the number.

    A. seventeen _____

    B. nine _____

4. What is the value of the coins?

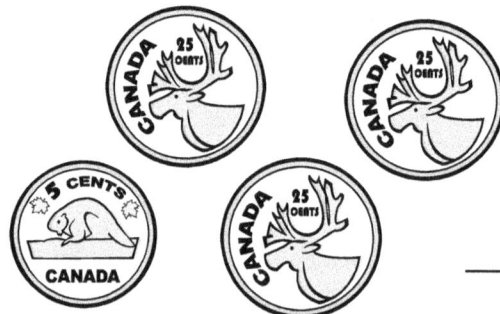

    _____ ¢

WEDNESDAY Geometry

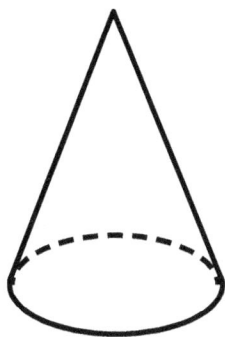

1. Circle the name of this 3D shape.

    cone   pyramid

2. How many edges does it have? _____

3. How many faces does it have? _____

4. Draw a triangle.

5. What a shape is inside the square?

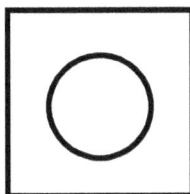

    A. circle
    B. square

THURSDAY Measurement

1. Write the time in two ways.

    _____ : _____

    quarter past _____

2. What is the better estimate of the weight of a crayon?

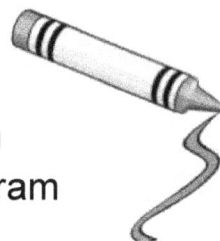

    A. 1 gram
    B. 1 kilogram

3. What day of the week is just after Thursday?

    A. Monday
    B. Tuesday
    C. Friday

4. Measure the length of the line.

    It is about _____ ⊂ long.

Data Management

Use the calendar to answer the questions.

June

Sunday	Monday	Tuesday	Wednesday	Thursday	Friday	Saturday
			1	2	3	4
5	6	7	8	9	10	11
12	13	14	15	16	17	18
18	20	21	22	23	24	25
26	27	28	29	30		

1. How many days are there in the month of June? _____

2. What day of the week is June 20th? _____

3. How many Thursdays are in June? _____

4. What day of the week will July start on? _____

BRAIN STRETCH

1.
```
   26
 + 32
 ____
```

2.
```
   71
 + 36
 ____
```

3.
```
   43
 − 12
 ____
```

4.
```
   98
 − 35
 ____
```

MONDAY Patterning and Algebra

1. What is the missing number to complete the number sentence?

   $9 - 6 = 2 +$ _____

2. How many circles are there in all? Add the rows. Write the addition equation.

   ___ + ___ + ___ + ___ = ___

3. Make a pattern using ◯ and ▢ .

   _____

   Explain your pattern rule. _____

TUESDAY Number Sense and Operations

1. What is the number?

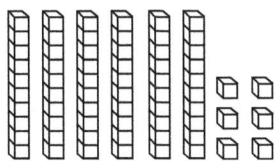

   tens _____
   ones _____
   number _____

2. Colour $\frac{5}{6}$ of the shape.

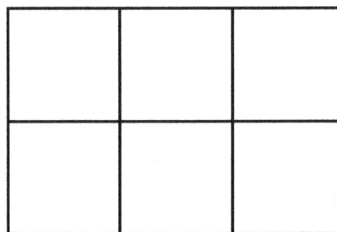

3. Write the numbers.

   A. nineteen _____

   B. eleven _____

4. What is the value of the coins?

   _____ ¢

WEDNESDAY Geometry

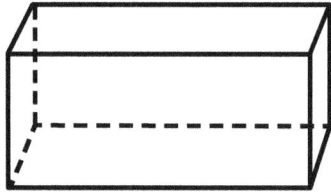

1. Circle the name of this 3D shape.

   rectangular prism   pyramid

2. How many edges does it have? _____

3. How many faces does it have? _____

4. Draw a square.

5. What shape is inside the triangle?

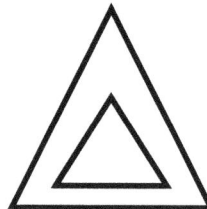

   A. triangle
   B. square

THURSDAY Measurement

1. Write the time in two ways.

   _____ : _____

   quarter past _____

2. About how wide is your finger?

   A. 1 metre
   B. 1 centimetre

3. What day of the week is just before Sunday?

   A. Saturday
   B. Tuesday
   C. Friday

4. What is a better estimate for the length of a truck?

   A. 16 metres
   B. 16 millimetres

Here are the results of a Favourite Season Survey.
Use the data from the pictograph to make a bar graph. Answer the questions.

Favourite Season

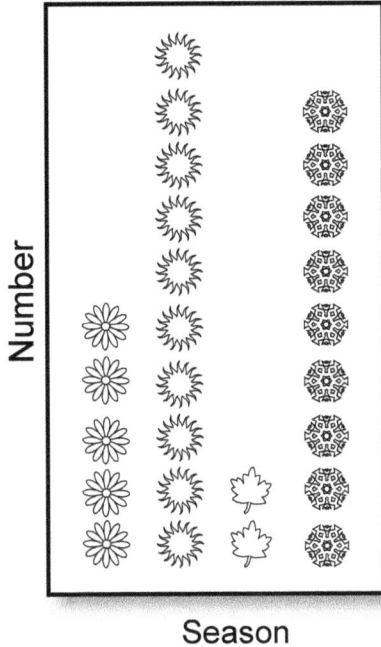

Season

Favourite Season Graph

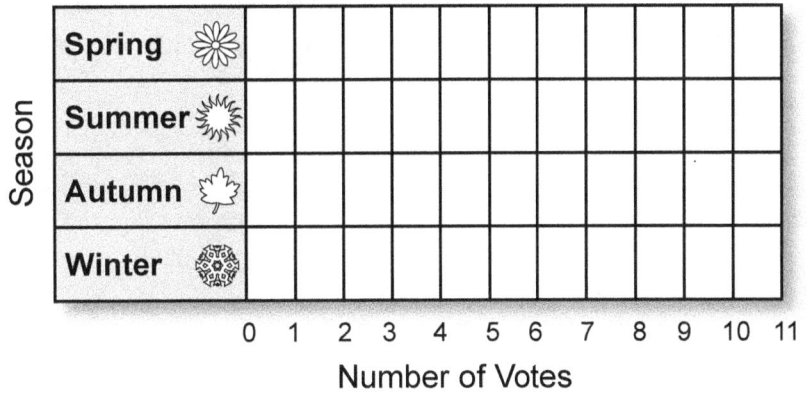

Season	0 1 2 3 4 5 6 7 8 9 10 11
Spring ✿	
Summer ☀	
Autumn 🍁	
Winter ❄	

Number of Votes

1. How many people voted for spring and summer? _____

2. How many more people voted for winter than spring? _____

3. Which season had the least number of votes? _____

4. How many people voted for winter and summer? _____

BRAIN STRETCH

1.
```
  42
+ 17
____
```

2.
```
  69
+ 11
____
```

3.
```
  89
- 28
____
```

4.
```
  70
- 30
____
```

MONDAY — Patterning and Algebra

1. What is the missing sign?

    3 _____ 12 = 15

2. What is the next number if the pattern rule is add 5?

    11, _____

3. Make an AB pattern using ◯ and ♡. Circle the core of the pattern.

    _____

4. Count on by 2s from 88.

    88, _____, _____, _____, _____

TUESDAY — Number Sense and Operations

1. Draw a model for 63 using

    | ten   ● one

2. Is 5 an odd or an even number?

    _____

    Pair the circles and explain your thinking.

    _____

    ◯ ◯ ◯ ◯ ◯

3. Colour 2/4 of the shape.

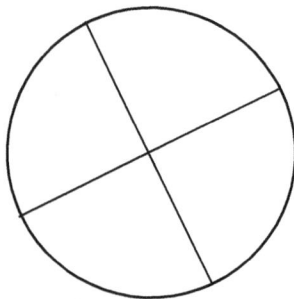

4. What is the value of the coins?

    _____ . _____ ¢

WEDNESDAY Geometry

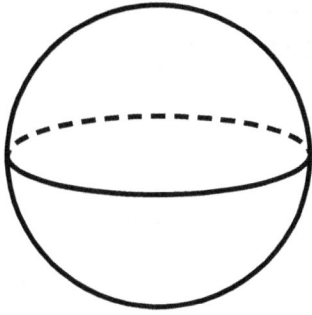

1. Circle the name of this 3D shape.

    cylinder   sphere

2. How many edges does it have? _____

3. How many faces does it have? _____

4. Draw a rectangle.

5. What shape is beside the square?

    A. triangle
    B. square

THURSDAY Measurement

1. Write the time in two ways.

    _____ : _____

    quarter past _____

2. How many days in two weeks?

    _____

3. How many weeks are there in a year?

    _____ weeks

4. Measure the length of the line.

    It is about _____ ◯ long.

Here are the results of a Favourite Breakfast Food Survey.
Complete the chart and answer the questions about the results.

Favourite Breakfast Food

Favourite Breakfast Foods	Tally	Number
Cereal		5
Eggs		10
Pancakes		6
Granola		6

1. What was the most popular breakfast food? _____

2. How many people liked either cereal or pancakes? _____

3. Which breakfast foods did people like the same? _____

4. What was the least popular breakfast food? _____

BRAIN STRETCH

1.
```
   13
 + 76
_____
```

2.
```
   32
 + 47
_____
```

3.
```
   98
 − 27
_____
```

4.
```
   81
 − 30
_____
```

MONDAY Patterning and Algebra

1. Write = or ≠ to make the number sentence true.

   $15 - 9$ ☐ $5 + 7$

2. What is the next number if the pattern rule is subtract 2?

   10, _____

3. What is the missing number to make the equation true?

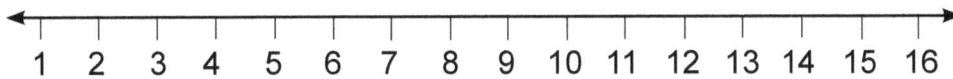

   $\xleftarrow{\hspace{1em}}$ 1 2 3 4 5 6 7 8 9 10 11 12 13 14 15 16 $\xrightarrow{\hspace{1em}}$

   $2 + 7 + 3 =$ _____ $+ 6 + 1$

TUESDAY Number Sense and Operations

1. Draw a model for 79 using

   | ten   ● one

2 Circle the value of the underlined digit.

   A. 6<u>7</u>   70   7

   B. <u>3</u>5   30   3

3. Is the number odd or even? Count by 2s to find out.

   A. 14 _____

   B. 5 _____

4. What is the value of the coins?

   _____ ¢

WEDNESDAY Geometry

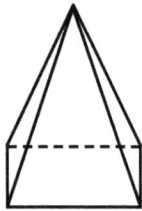

1. Circle the name of this 3D shape.

   cylinder   pyramid

2. How many edges does it have? _____

3. How many faces does it have? _____

4. Draw a pentagon.

5. What shape is under the circle?

   A. triangle
   B. square

THURSDAY Measurement

1. Compare the lengths.
   Which length is equal to the line?

   _____

   A.

   B.

2. What month of the year comes right after January?

   _____

3. How many days are there in a year?

   _____ days

4. Draw a line 5 centimetres long.

Here are the results of a Favourite Drink Survey.
Use the pictograph to answer the questions about the results.

Favourite Drink

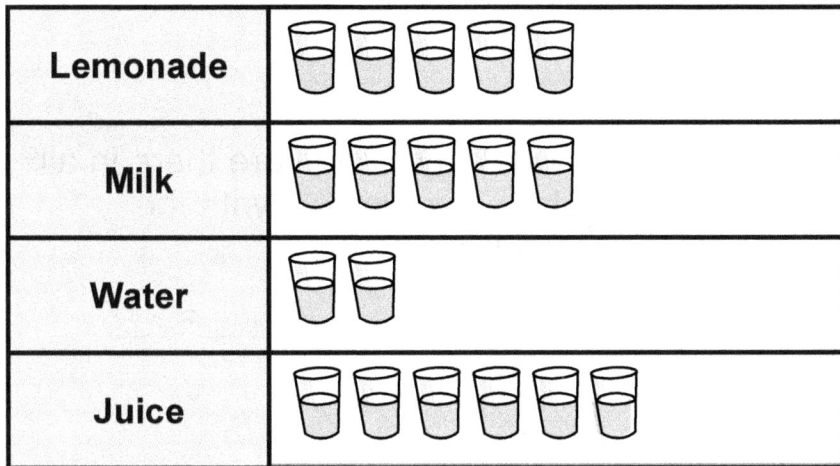

Each  stands for 2 votes.

1. What drink do people like the most? _____

2. What drink do people like the least? _____

3. How many people voted in this survey? _____

4. Which two drinks did people like the same? _____

BRAIN STRETCH

There were 37 students in the gym. 14 more students came into the gym.
How many students are in the gym? Use the number line to help solve.

_____ students

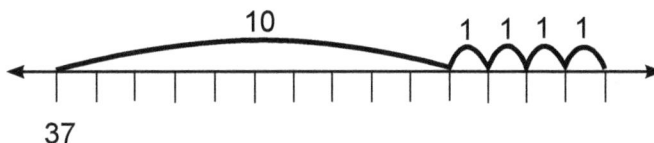

MONDAY — Patterning and Algebra

1. Write = or ≠ to make the number sentence true.

   5 + 12 ▢ 10 + 10

2. What is the next number if the pattern rule is add 3?

   4, _____

3. What is the missing number to make the equation true?

   1 + 7 + _____ = 4 + 4 + 4

4. How many circles are there in all? Add the columns. Write the equation.

   ___ + ___ + ___ + ___ = ___

   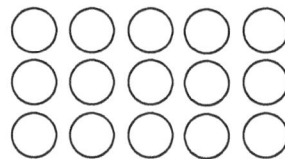

TUESDAY — Number Sense and Operations

1. What is the number?

   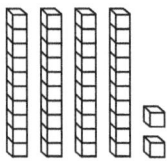

   tens _____

   ones _____

   number _____

2. Order the numbers from the greatest to least.

   73, 21, 17

   _____ > _____ > _____

3. What are two related facts for 5 + 3 = 8?

   _____ + _____ = _____

   _____ − _____ = _____

4. Colour $\frac{1}{2}$ of the shape.

   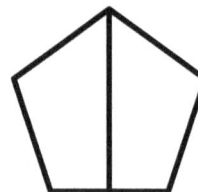

WEDNESDAY Geometry

1. Colour the shapes that are the same size and shape.

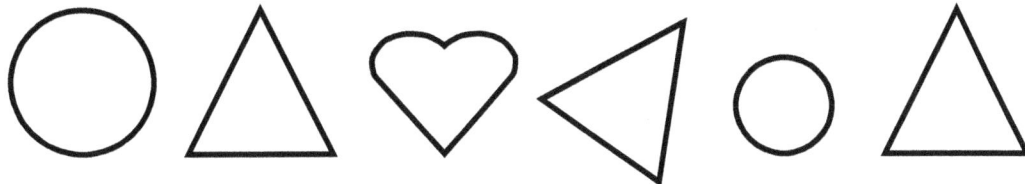

○ △ ♡ ◁ ○ △

2. Draw a hexagon.

3. What shape is above the square?

△

□

A. triangle

B. square

THURSDAY Measurement

1. Write the time in two ways.

_____ : _____

quarter past _____

2. Circle the better estimate of the length of a strawberry.

A. 1 centimetre

B. 1 metre

3. Is the temperature hot or cold?

A. hot

B. cold

4. Measure the length of the line.

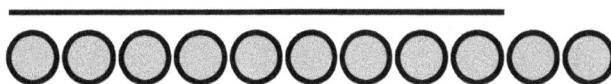

○○○○○○○○○○○○

It is about _____ ○ long.

FRIDAY Data Management

Use the Venn diagram to answer the questions about these students' favourite recess activities.

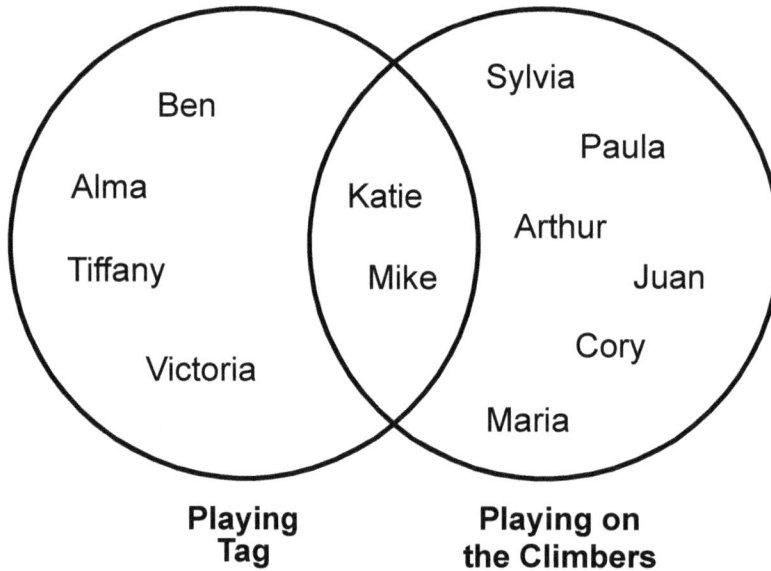

Favourite Recess Activities

Ben, Alma, Tiffany, Victoria

Katie, Mike

Sylvia, Paula, Arthur, Juan, Cory, Maria

Playing Tag   **Playing on the Climbers**

1. Which students like to play tag, but not play on the climbers?

_____

2. Which students like to play on the climbers, but not play tag?

_____

3. Which students like to do both activities?

_____

BRAIN STRETCH

1. 45
   + 39

2. 61
   + 29

3. 70
   − 44

4. 35
   − 19

MONDAY — Patterning and Algebra

1. Write = or ≠ to make the number sentence true.

   $14 - 7$ [ ] $12 - 5$

2. What is the next number if the pattern rule is subtract 7?

   14, _____

3. What is the missing number to make the equation true?

   $2 + 5 +$ _____ $= 3 + 3 + 3$

4. What is the missing number in this sequence?

   _____, 20, 15, 10, 5

TUESDAY — Number Sense and Operations

1. Draw a model for 95 using

   | ten   ● one

2. What are two related facts for $7 + 5 = 12$?

   _____ + _____ = _____

   _____ − _____ = _____

3. Write the number.

   A. $10 + 2 =$ _____

   B. $40 + 1 =$ _____

4. Colour $\frac{1}{3}$ of the shape.

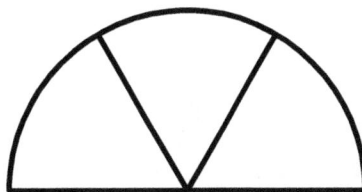

WEDNESDAY Geometry

1. Colour the shapes that are the same size and shape.

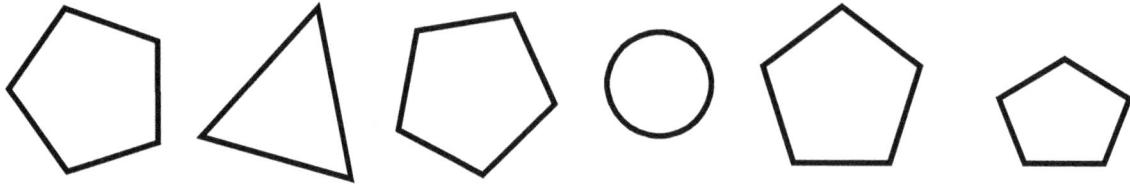

2. Draw an octagon.

3. What shape is inside the triangle?

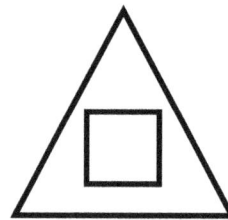

   A. circle

   B. square

THURSDAY Measurement

1. Write the time in two ways.

   _____ : _____

   quarter to _____

2. Compare the lengths.
   Which length is longer than the line?

   _____

   A.

   B.

3. Which tree is taller?

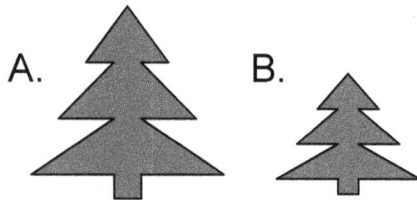

   A.   B.

4. Measure the length of the line.

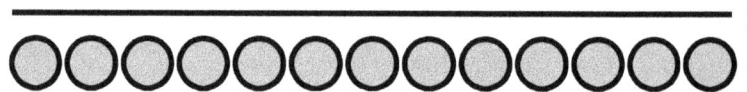

   It is about _____ ◯ long.

Data Management

Use the Venn diagram to answer the questions about these students' favourite snack foods.

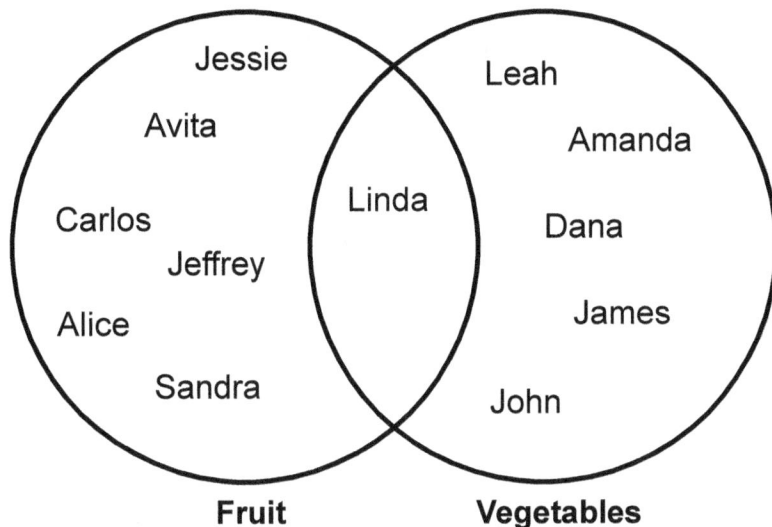

Favourite Snack Foods

Jessie

Avita

Carlos

Jeffrey

Alice

Sandra

Linda

Leah

Amanda

Dana

James

John

Fruit   **Vegetables**

1. Which students like fruit, but not vegetables?

_____

2. Which students like to eat vegetables as a snack?

_____

3. Which students like vegetables, but not fruit?

_____

BRAIN STRETCH

1.	2.	3.	4.
37 + 58	29 + 46	65 − 37	58 − 29

MONDAY — Patterning and Algebra

1. Write = or ≠ to make the number sentence true.

   8 – 4 [ ] 10 – 6

2. Is this a growing, shrinking, or repeating pattern?

3. Create a number pattern. _____

   What is your rule? _____

4. Count back by 1s.

   45, 44, 43, _____, _____, _____

TUESDAY — Number Sense and Operations

1. What is the value of the underlined digit?

   A. 2<u>7</u>1 _____

   B. <u>3</u>69 _____

2. Show the fewest coins to make 75 cents.

3. How many tens and ones in 63?

   tens _____

   ones _____

4. Circle $\frac{1}{2}$ of the group.

WEDNESDAY Geometry

1. Colour the cube red.
   Colour the cone green.

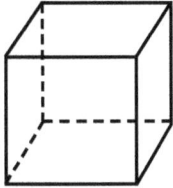

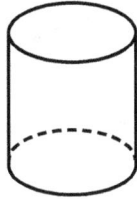

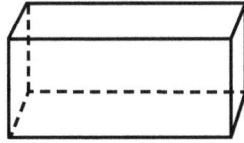

   Colour the cylinder yellow.
   Colour the rectangular prism blue.

2. What is the name of
   this 3D shape?

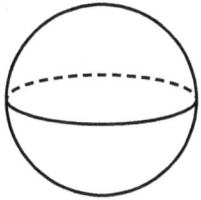

   A. sphere
   B. pyramid

3. What shape is under the circle?

   A. octagon
   B. rectangle

THURSDAY Measurement

1. Draw in the hands on the
   clock to show the time 11:45.

2. One cricket jumped up 9 centimetres.
   Another cricket jumped up
   13 centimetres. How much higher did the
   second cricket jump?

   9 + __ = 13   ____ centimetres higher

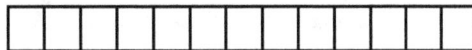

3. Choose the better unit of
   measure for the capacity
   of a large jug of juice.

   A. millilitre
   B. litre

4. Measure the length of the line.

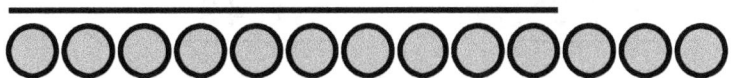

   It is about _____ ◯ long.

FRIDAY Data Management

Use the Venn diagram to answer the questions about these students' favourite school clubs.

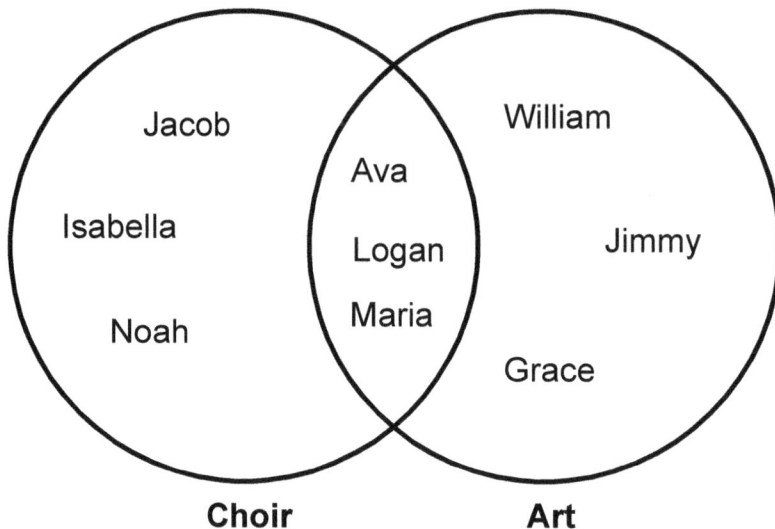

Favourite School Clubs

Jacob

Isabella

Noah

Ava

Logan

Maria

William

Jimmy

Grace

Choir   **Art**

1. Which students are in the choir, but not the art club?

_____

2. Which students are in the art club, but not in the choir?

_____

3. How many students are in both?

_____

BRAIN STRETCH

1.
$$\begin{array}{r} 64 \\ + 26 \\ \hline \end{array}$$

2.
$$\begin{array}{r} 38 \\ + 49 \\ \hline \end{array}$$

3.
$$\begin{array}{r} 56 \\ - 32 \\ \hline \end{array}$$

4.
$$\begin{array}{r} 94 \\ - 58 \\ \hline \end{array}$$

1. Find the sum.

   5 + 7 + 8 =

2. What is the next number if the pattern rule is subtract 10?

   35, _____

3. Is this a growing, shrinking or repeating pattern?

   _____

4. What is the missing number in this pattern?

   22, 32, 22, 32, 22, _____ , 22, 32, 22

TUESDAY — Number Sense and Operations

1. What is the value of the underlined digit?

   A. 7<u>8</u> _____

   B. 4<u>9</u> _____

2. What are two related facts for 16 – 7 = 9?

   _____ + _____ = _____

   _____ – _____ = _____

3. Write the number in expanded form.

   A. 38 = _____

   B. 29 = _____

4. Colour $\frac{1}{2}$ of the shape.

   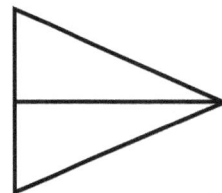

WEDNESDAY Geometry

1. Colour the cylinder green.
   Colour the cone red.
   Colour the sphere orange.
   Colour the cube blue.

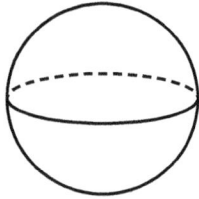

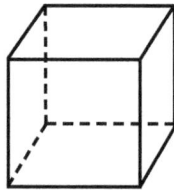

2. What is the name of this 3D shape?

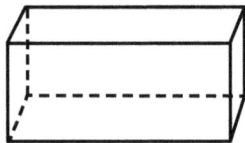

   A. rectangular prism

   B. cone

3. Draw a line of symmetry on the shape.

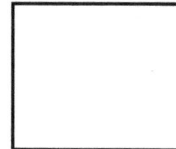

THURSDAY Measurement

1. Write the time in two ways.

   _____ : _____

   quarter past _____

2. What is a better estimate of the weight of a bicycle?

   A. about 1 kilogram

   B. more than 1 kilogram

   C. less than 1 kilogram

3. Draw a line 9 cm long.

4. What is the month just before June?

   _____

Use the Venn diagram to answer the questions about these students' favourite treats.

Favourite Treats

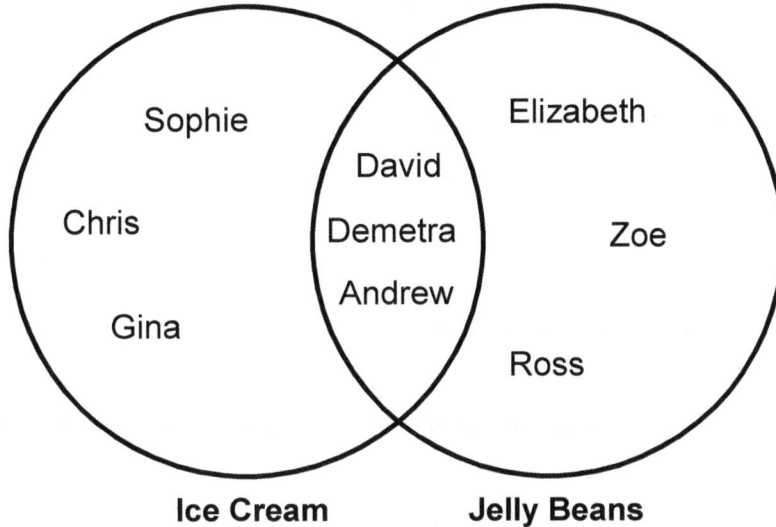

Sophie

Chris

Gina

David

Demetra

Andrew

Elizabeth

Zoe

Ross

Ice Cream   **Jelly Beans**

1. Which students like ice cream but not jelly beans?

_____

2. How many students like jelly beans?

_____

3. Which students like ice cream and jelly beans?

_____

BRAIN STRETCH

There were 36 puppies. 17 puppies were adopted. How many puppies are left? Use the number line.

$36 - 17 =$ ___

___ puppies

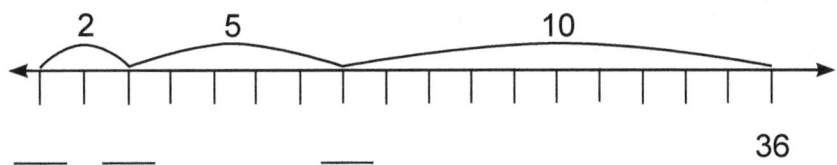

2   5   10

___ ___   ___   36

MONDAY Patterning and Algebra

1. Find the difference.

   $18 - 5 - 3 =$ _____

2. What is the next number if the pattern rule is add 9?

   21, _____

3. Is this a growing, shrinking, or repeating pattern?

   90, 80, 70, 60

   _____

4. Create a pattern where only colour changes. Circle the core of the pattern.

   _____

TUESDAY Number Sense and Operations

1. Find the missing sign.

   31 $\bigcirc$ 12

   A. <   B. =   C. >

2. What are two related facts for $13 - 5 = 8$?

   _____ + _____ = _____

   _____ − _____ = _____

3. Tell if the numbers are odd or even.

   A. 19 _____

   B. 7 _____

4. Colour $\frac{1}{4}$ of the shape.

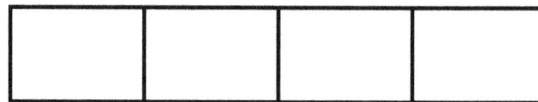

Week 20

1. Colour the cylinder red.   Colour the pyramid green.
   Colour the cube blue.   Colour the sphere orange.

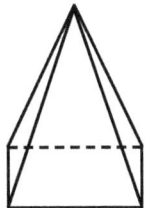

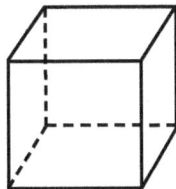

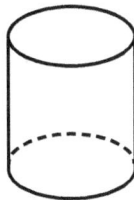

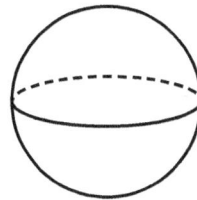

2. What is the name of
   this 3D shape?

   A. sphere
   B. cone

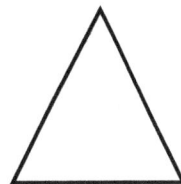

3. Draw a line of symmetry
   on the shape.

THURSDAY Measurement

1. Write the time in two ways.

   _____ : _____

   quarter past _____

2. What month comes just after
   October?

   _____

3. What is the better estimate
   of the length of a bug?

   A. 2 metres
   B. 2 centimetres

4. Janie is 44 centimetres tall. Her
   baby sister is 18 centimetres tall.
   How much taller is Janie than her
   sister? Show your work.

   $44 - 18 =$ ☐

   _____ centimetres taller

Data Management

Use the calendar to answer the questions.

July

Sunday	Monday	Tuesday	Wednesday	Thursday	Friday	Saturday
		1	2	3	4	5
6	7	8	9	10	11	12
13	14	15	16	17	18	19
20	21	22	23	24	25	26
27	28	29	30	31		

1. How many days are there in the month of July? _____

2. What day of the week is July 12th? _____

3. What day of the week is July 21st? _____

4. What day of the week does the month end on? _____

BRAIN STRETCH

Draw 3 irregular shapes with 4 sides.

MONDAY   Patterning and Algebra

1. Find the difference.

   $16 - 4 - 1 =$ _____

2. There were 9 rabbits in the garden. 11 more rabbits came. How many rabbits were in the garden? Use pictures and an equation to show your work.

   _____

3. Colour a pattern.

   _____ rabbits

   What is your pattern rule? _____

TUESDAY   Number Sense and Operations

1. Find the missing sign.

   42 (   ) 42

   A. <   B. =   C. >

2. Estimate the sum.
   Choose the better choice.

   $24 + 15 =$ _____

   A. greater than 50
   B. less than 50

4. Show the fewest coins to make 90¢.

4. Circle $\frac{1}{3}$ of the group.

WEDNESDAY Geometry

1. Colour the shapes with more than 3 vertices green.

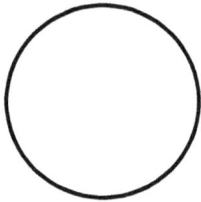

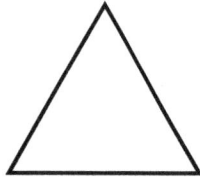

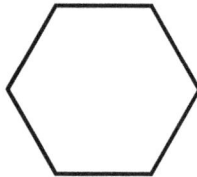

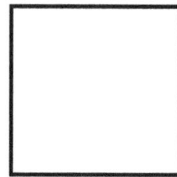

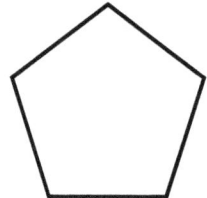

2. What is the name of this 3D shape?

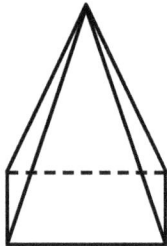

   A. sphere

   B. pyramid

3. Draw a line of symmetry on the shape.

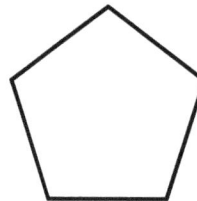

THURSDAY Measurement

1. Write the time in two ways.

   _____ : _____

   quarter to _____

2. Tori went to visit her aunt from 5:00 to 8:00. How long did she visit her aunt?

   _____ hours

3. What is the better estimate of the length of a car?

   A. 4 metres

   B. 4 centimetres

4. What measurement tool would you use to check the date?

   A. calendar

   B. measuring cup

   C. scale

Use the calendar to answer the questions.

November

Sunday	Monday	Tuesday	Wednesday	Thursday	Friday	Saturday
				1	2	3
4	5	6	7	8	9	10
11	12	13	14	15	16	17
18	19	20	21	22	23	24
25	26	27	28	29	30	

1. How many days are there in the month of November? _____

2. What day of the week is November 16th? _____

3. What day of the week is November 20th _____

4. What day of the week will December start on? _____

BRAIN STRETCH

Anna has three dogs, four cats, six hamsters and one bird.
How many pets does she have altogether?

MONDAY — Patterning and Algebra

1. What is the missing number?

    _____ + 10 = 13

2. What is the next number if the pattern rule is subtract 4?

    19, _____

3. Create a pattern where only shape changes. Circle the core of the pattern. .

    _____

TUESDAY — Number Sense and Operations

1. Estimate the sum. Choose the better choice.

    28 + 51 = _____

    A. greater than 50
    B. less than 50

2. Colour $\frac{2}{6}$ of the shape.

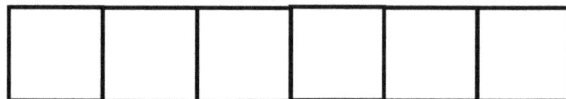

3. What is the difference?

    $$\begin{array}{r} 92 \\ -\ 25 \\ \hline \end{array}$$

4. Circle $\frac{1}{4}$ of the group.

© Chalkboard Publishing

WEDNESDAY Geometry

1. Colour the shapes with more than 5 vertices red.

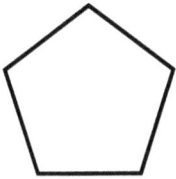

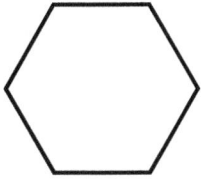

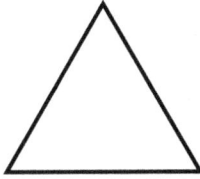

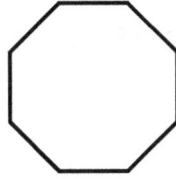

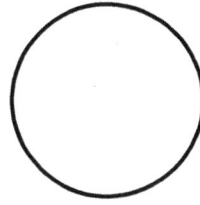

2. Can this 3D shape be stacked?

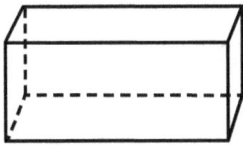

   A. yes
   B. no

3. Draw a line of symmetry on the shape.

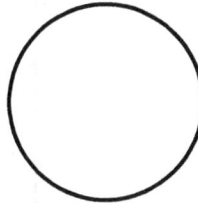

THURSDAY Measurement

1. Write the time in two ways.

   _____ : _____

   quarter past _____

2. How many centimetres in a metre?

   There are _____ centimetres in a metre.

3. The rectangle was divided into 2 rows and 3 columns. How many squares are there?

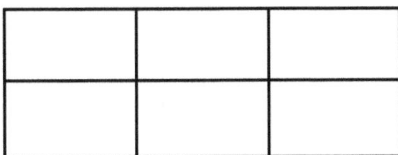

   _____ squares

4. Divide the rectangle. Make 2 rows and 4 columns. Check that the squares are the same size. Count the squares.

   _____ squares

Here are the results of a Favourite Meal Survey.
Answer the questions using the information from the bar graph.

Favourite Meal Graph

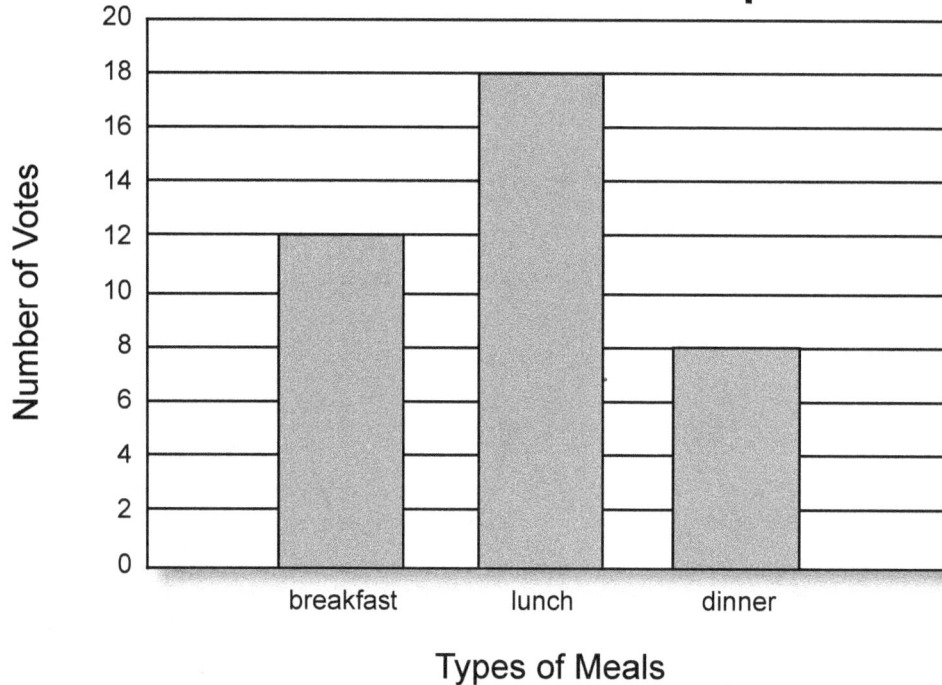

Number of Votes (vertical axis: 0, 2, 4, 6, 8, 10, 12, 14, 16, 18, 20)

breakfast — 12
lunch — 18
dinner — 8

Types of Meals

1. What is this graph about? _____

2. Which meal got 8 votes? _____

3. Which meal was the most popular? _____

4. Which meal was the least popular? _____

BRAIN STRETCH

There were 37 frogs at the pond. 19 frogs jumped away.
How many frogs were left?

MONDAY   Patterning and Algebra

1. Write = or ≠ to make the number sentence true.

$1 + 11$ ☐ $12 - 1$

2. What is the missing number to make the equation true?

$10 + 3 = 2 + _____$

3. Colour a pattern. Circle the core of the pattern.

◇ ◇ ◇ ◇ ◇ ◇ ◇ ◇

What is your pattern rule? _____

TUESDAY   Number Sense and Operations

1. Compare the numbers using <, >, or =.

36 ◯ 36

A. <   B. =   C. >

2. Sasha solved 45 + 25. She added 40 + 20 + 5 + 5.

Is her strategy correct? _____

Show how you know.

$40 + 20 = \_\_\_$ $5 + 5 = \_\_\_$

$60 + 10 = \_\_\_$ So, $45 + 25 = \_\_\_$.

3. Subtract:

A. $60 - 10 = _____$

B. $90 - 20 = _____$

4. What are two related facts for $8 + 5 = 13$?

_____ + _____ = _____

_____ − _____ = _____

WEDNESDAY Geometry

1. Colour the quadrilaterals red.

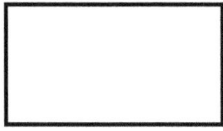

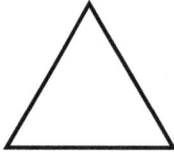

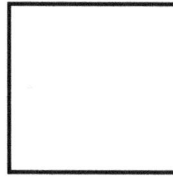

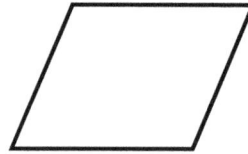

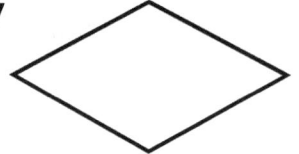

2. Can this 3D shape be stacked?

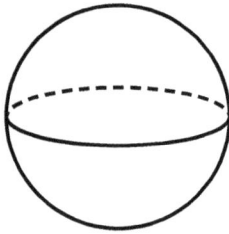

   A. yes
   B. no

3. Draw a line of symmetry on the shape.

THURSDAY Measurement

1. Write the time in two ways.

   _____ : _____

   quarter to _____

2. What is the better estimate of the width of a window?

   A. 10 centimetres
   B. 1 metre

3. Divide the rectangle. Make 3 rows and 2 columns. Count the squares.

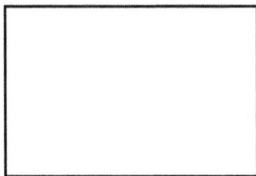

   _____ squares

4. Count the squares.

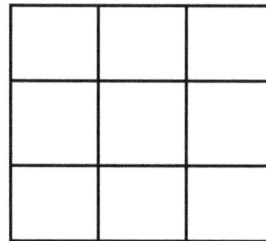

   _____ squares

Here are the results of a Favourite Fruit Survey.
Answer the questions using the information from the bar graph.

Favourite Fruit

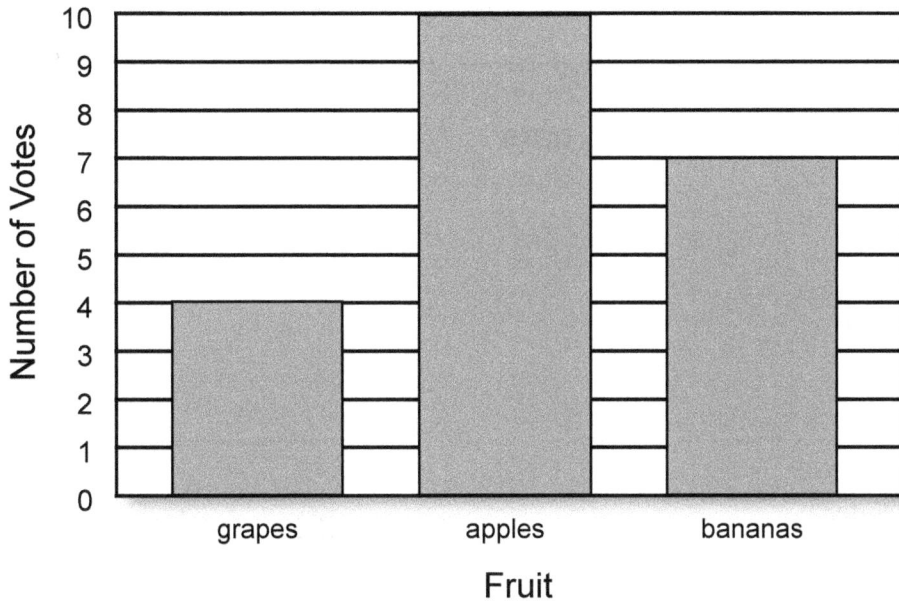

1. What fruit was the most popular? _____

2. What fruit was the least popular? _____

3. Order the fruits from the least number of votes to the most.

   _____

4. How many votes were there for grapes and bananas? _____

5. How many more votes were there for apples than grapes? _____

BRAIN STRETCH

Maria had 35 jelly beans. She bought 57 more.
How many jelly beans does Maria have altogether?

MONDAY — Patterning and Algebra

1. What is the sum?

    $26 + 5 =$ _____

2. There are 3 red cars, 12 blue cars, and 4 green cars in the parking lot. How many cars are in the lot? Draw a picture and write an equation to help you.

    _____

    _____ cars

3. What is the difference?

    $67 - 8 =$ _____

4. Create a number pattern.

    _____

    What is your pattern rule? _____

TUESDAY — Number Sense and Operations

1. Compare the numbers using <, >, or =.

    43 ◯ 33

    A. <   B. =   C. >

2. Colour 3/5 of the shape.

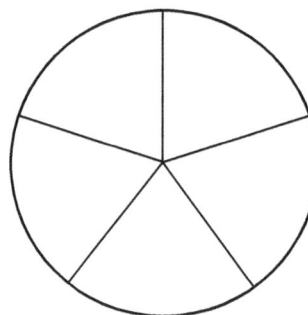

3. Write the numbers.

    A. seven _____

    B. four _____

    C. eleven _____

4. Circle $\frac{1}{2}$ of the group.

WEDNESDAY Geometry

1. Colour the shapes with fewer than 6 vertices green.

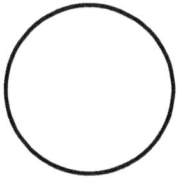

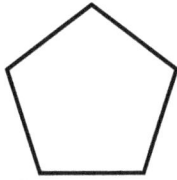

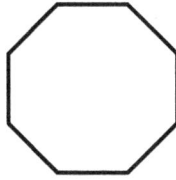

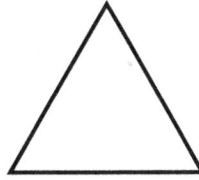

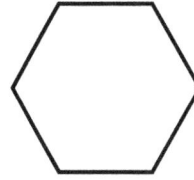

2. Can this 3D shape roll?

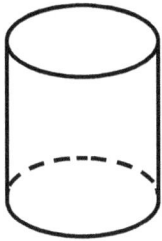

   A. yes
   B. no

3. What shape is outside the parallelogram?

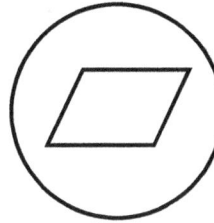

   A. pentagon
   B. circle

THURSDAY Measurement

1. What time will it be in 2 hours?

   _____ : _____

2. Draw a line 5 centimetres long.

3. The rectangle has ___ equal parts.
   There are ___ fourths altogether.
   Each part is called one _____.

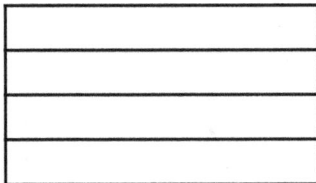

   _____ units

4. How many squares are there?

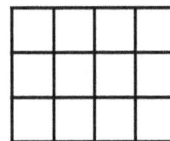

   _____ squares

Here are the results of a Favourite Music Survey.
Answer the questions using the information from the bar graph.

Favourite Music

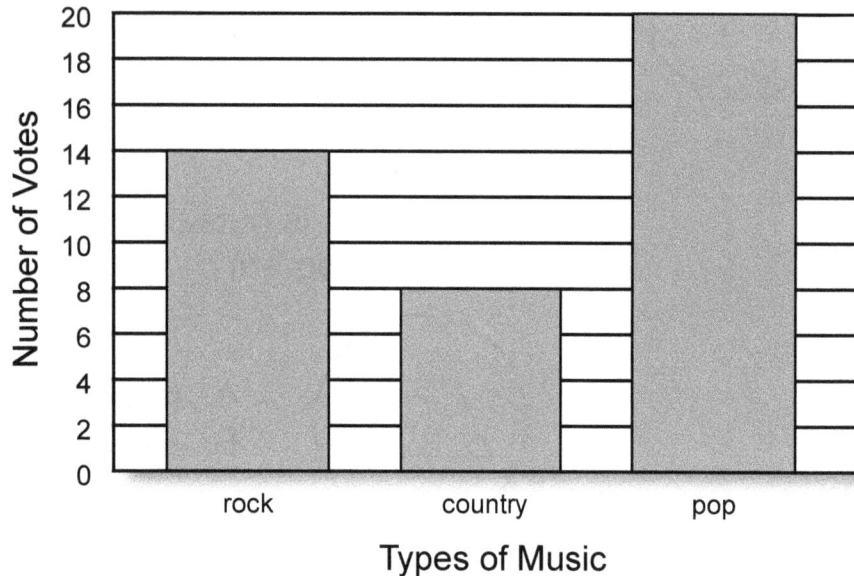

Number of Votes

Types of Music

1. What music was the most popular? _____

2. What music was the least popular? _____

3. Order the types of music from the most number of votes to the least.

   _____

4. How many votes were there for rock and country? _____

5. How many fewer votes were there for country than pop? _____

BRAIN STRETCH

Chris had 67 hockey cards. He gave 19 cards to Stephen.
How many hockey cards does Chris have left?

MONDAY — Patterning and Algebra

1. What is the sum?

    $33 + 9 = $ _____

2. What is the difference?

    $81 - 5 = $ _____

3. Count on by 10s.

    540, 550, _____, _____, _____, _____, _____

4. Create a pattern where only shape changes. Circle the core of the pattern.

    _____

TUESDAY — Number Sense and Operations

1. Use the number line to choose the number that completes the sentence.

    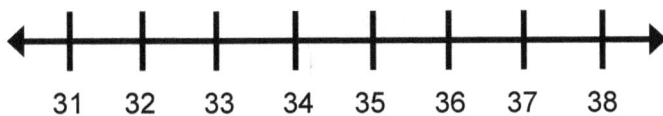

    31   32   33   34   35   36   37   38

    36 is two more than _____

2. List the numbers from greatest to least.

    85, 76, 90

    _____ > _____ > _____

3. Add.

    A. $20 + 30 = $ _____

    B. $60 + 30 = $ _____

4. Circle the fourth unicorn.

WEDNESDAY Geometry

1. Colour the octagons red.   Colour the trapezoid green.
   Colour the pentagons yellow. Colour the rectangles blue.

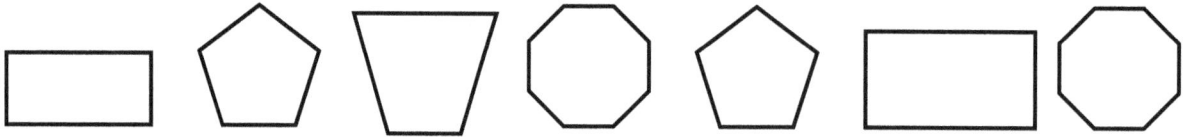

2. Can this 3D shape roll?

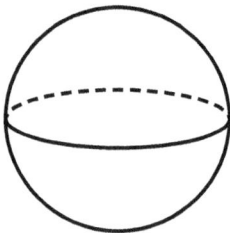

   A. yes
   B. no

3. Draw a line of symmetry on the shape.

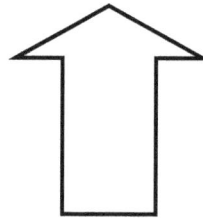

THURSDAY Measurement

1. Draw in the hands on the clock to show the time 10:25.

2. What month is just after September?

   A. December

   B. October

   C. April

3. Count the squares.

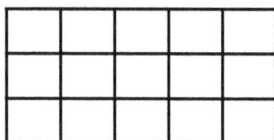

   _____ squares

4. Divide the rectangle into 2 equal parts.
   There are ____ halves altogether.
   Each part is called one _____.

Here are the results of a Favourite School Subject Survey.
Use the data from the chart to make a bar graph. Answer the questions.

Favourite School Subject

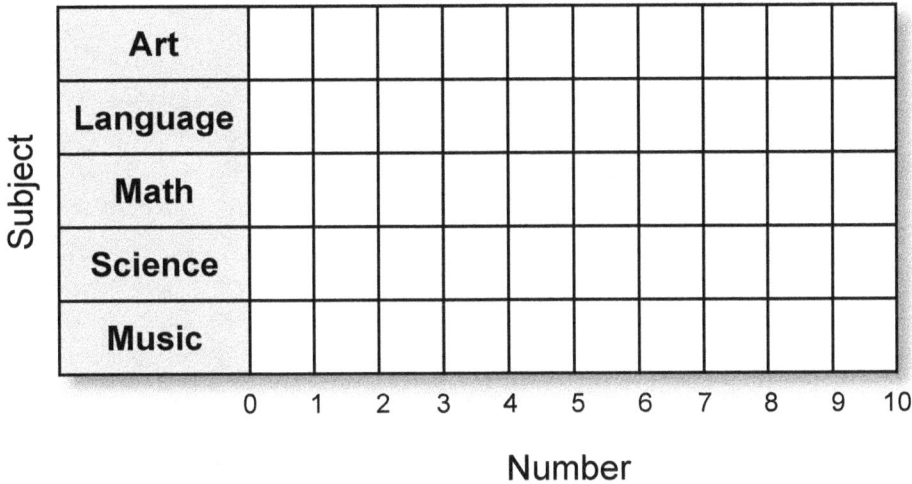

Subject											
Art											
Language											
Math											
Science											
Music											

0 1 2 3 4 5 6 7 8 9 10

Number

Favourite School Subject

School Subject	Number
Art	6
Language	9
Math	8
Science	8
Music	4

1. What was the most popular subject? _____

2. How many voted for art and math? _____

3. Which subjects had same number of votes? _____

BRAIN STRETCH

Cathy baked 24 chocolate chip cookies and 36 oatmeal raisin cookies.
How many cookies did Cathy bake in all?

MONDAY Patterning and Algebra

1. Count on by 10s from 150.

   150, _____, _____, _____, _____

2. What is the difference?

   $35 - 9 =$ _____

3. Jason has 9 oranges. Lucy has 17 oranges. How many more oranges does Lucy have than Jason. Use pictures and an equation to show your work.

   Lucy has _____ more oranges than Jason.

TUESDAY Number Sense and Operations

1. Use the number line to choose the number that completes the sentence.

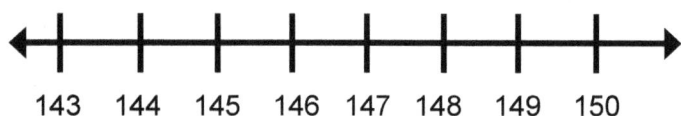

   143   144   145   146   147   148   149   150

   148 is one less than _____

2. Find the sum. Write the equation.

   6 groups of 2

   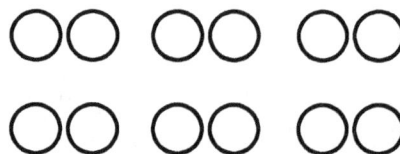

   _____

3. Subtract.

   A. $80 - 70 =$ _____

   B. $60 - 40 =$ _____

4. Circle the sixth elephant.

WEDNESDAY — Geometry

1. Look at the shapes.
   Choose flip, slide, or turn.

   A. flip   B. slide   C. turn

2. Look at the shapes.
   Choose flip, slide, or turn.

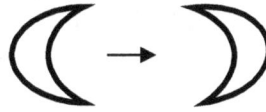

   A. flip   B. slide   C. turn

3. Can this 3D shape roll?

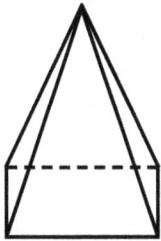

   A. yes
   B. no

4. Draw a line of symmetry on this letter.

H

THURSDAY — Measurement

1. Write the time in two ways.

   _____ : _____

   quarter to _____

2. Which is lighter?

A.    B.

3. What length is longer?

   A. 6 centimetres
   B. 6 metres

4. What is the area?

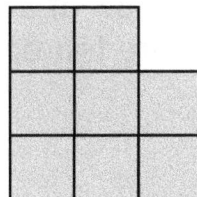

   _____ square units

FRIDAY Data Management

Here are the results of a Favourite Fair Ride Survey.
Answer the questions using the information from the bar graph.

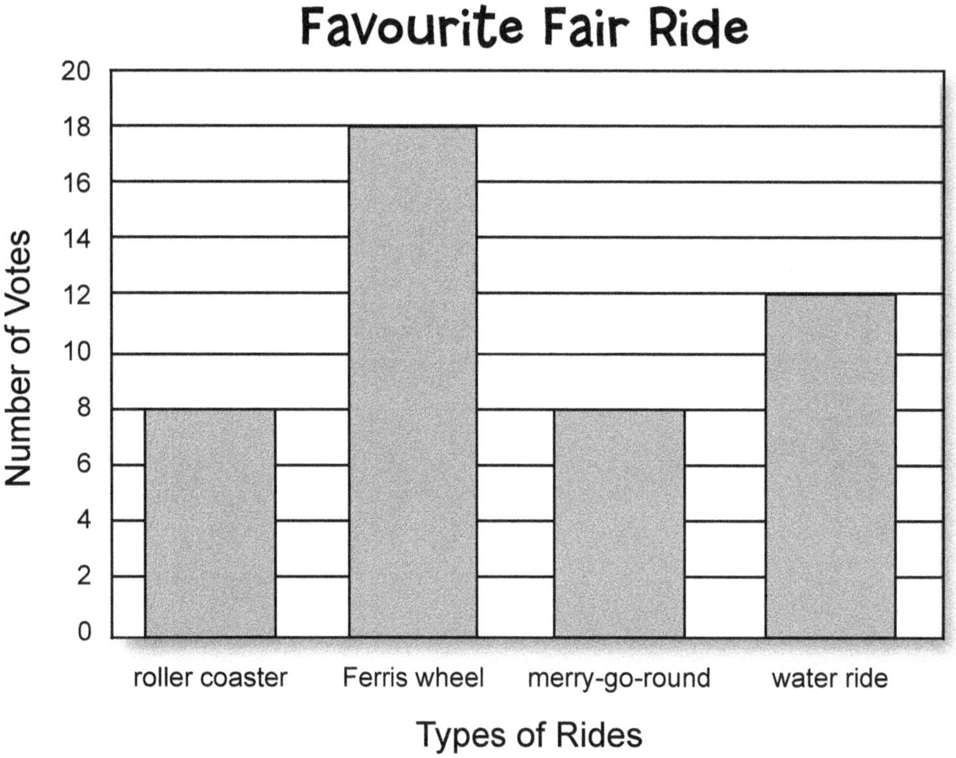

1. Which ride was the most popular? ____________________________

2. Which two rides had the same number of votes ? ________________________

3. How many more votes for the water ride than the roller coaster? _________

4. How many votes for the merry-go-round? ____________

BRAIN STRETCH

There were 81 ants on a log. 57 of the ants were eaten by an anteater. How many ants were left on the log?

MONDAY — Patterning and Algebra

1. Count on by 5s from 185.

   185, _____, _____, _____, _____

2. What is the difference?

   $61 - 9 =$ _____

3. Create a pattern where only size changes. Circle the core of the pattern.

   _____

4. Write = or ≠ to make the number sentence true.

   10 + 10 ☐ 18 – 1

TUESDAY — Number Sense and Operations

1. Draw 4 coins to make 80 cents.

2. Estimate the sum.
   Choose the better choice.

   $17 + 32 =$ _____

   A. greater than 50
   B. less than 50

3. Subtract.

   A. $9 - 5 =$ _____
   B. $90 - 50 =$ _____

4. What are two related facts for
   $14 - 5 = 9$?

   _____ + _____ = _____

   _____ – _____ = _____

WEDNESDAY Geometry

1. Colour the hexagons red.   Colour the circles blue.
   Colour the triangles yellow.   Colour the parallelogram green.

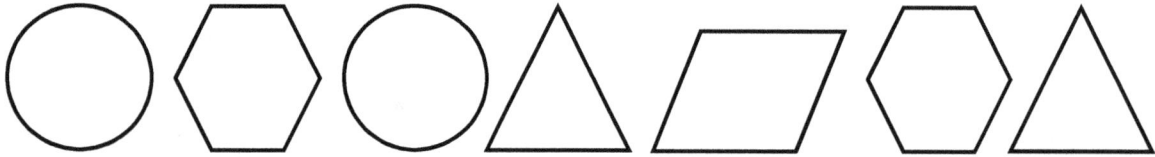

2. Can this 3D shape roll?

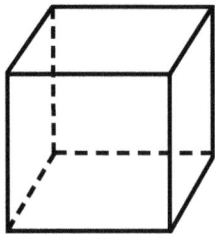

   A. yes
   B. no

3. What shape is above
   the parallelogram?

   A. pentagon
   B. circle

THURSDAY Measurement

1. Draw in the hands on the clock
   to show the time 2:45.

2. What month come just before August?

   _____

3. Draw a line 5 centimetres long.

4. What temperature does it need to
   be for rain to freeze?

   _____

Here are the results of a Favourite Colour Survey.
Answer the questions using the information from the tally chart.

Favourite Colour

Colour	Tally	Number
Red	ⵋⵋ IIII	
Blue	ⵋⵋ ⵋⵋ III	
Green	ⵋⵋ III	
Yellow	II	

1. What was the most popular colour? _____

2. What was the least popular colour? _____

3. How many people liked either green or yellow? _____

4. Order the colours from the most number of votes to the least.

_____

BRAIN STRETCH

Carlos has 5 dimes. He trades them with Mia for nickels.
How many nickels does Carlos now have?

MONDAY — Patterning and Algebra

1. What is the sum?

   $45 + 6 =$ _____

2. What is the difference?

   $72 - 4 =$ _____

3. Create a pattern where only colour changes. Circle the core of the pattern.

   _____

4. What is the missing number to complete the number sentence?

   _____ $- 4 = 7 + 3$

TUESDAY — Number Sense and Operations

1. Find the sum. Write the addition sentence.

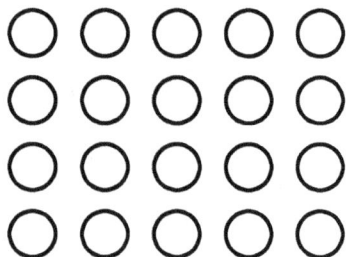

   ○ ○ ○ ○ ○
   ○ ○ ○ ○ ○
   ○ ○ ○ ○ ○
   ○ ○ ○ ○ ○

   _____

2. Estimate the sum. Choose the better choice.

   $16 + 22 =$ _____

   A. greater than 50
   B. less than 50

3. What are two related facts for $3 + 9 = 12$?

   _____ + _____ = _____

   _____ − _____ = _____

4. Colour $\frac{3}{4}$ of the shape.

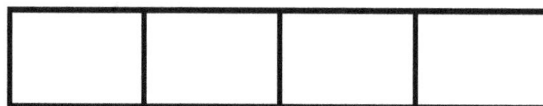

WEDNESDAY Geometry

1. Colour the pentagons red.   Colour the octagons orange.
   Colour the triangle blue.   Colour the trapezoids green.

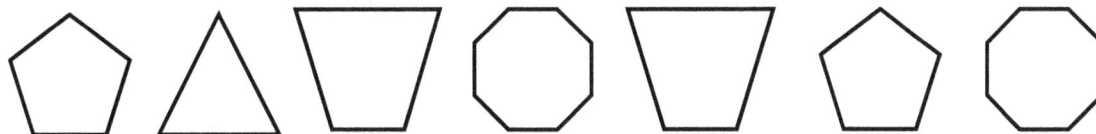

2. Look at the shapes.
   Choose flip, slide, or turn.

   A. flip   B. slide   C. turn

3. Draw a line of symmetry
   on this letter.

   A

THURSDAY Measurement

1. What time was it 1 hour ago?

   ____ : ____

2. What could be the
   temperature on a hot day?

   _____

3. Susie has 3 quarters and
   2 dimes. How many cents
   does she have? Use
   pictures and words.

   ___ cents

4. Compare the lengths.
   Which length is longer than the line?

   A.

   B.

Use the Venn diagram to answer the questions about these students' favourite circus performers.

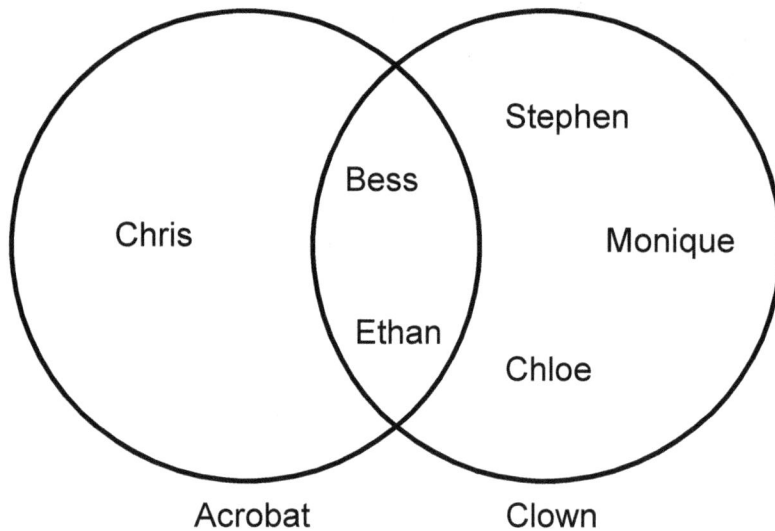

Favourite Circus Performer

Chris

Bess

Ethan

Stephen

Monique

Chloe

Acrobat   Clown

1. Which students like clowns, but not acrobats?

_____

2. Which students like acrobats?

_____

3. Which students like clowns and acrobats?

_____

BRAIN STRETCH

Lisa bought 3 boxes of cupcakes. Each box has 4 cupcakes.
How many cupcakes does Lisa have altogether?

MONDAY — Patterning and Algebra

1. What is the sum?

   $22 + 8 =$ _____

2. What is the difference?

   $43 - 10 =$ _____

3. Create a number pattern.

   _____

   What is your pattern rule?

   _____

4. There were some students in the gym. Then 14 more students came. There are now 37 students. How many students were in the gym at the start?

   _____

TUESDAY — Number Sense and Operations

1. Find the sum. Write the addition sentence.

   _____

   ○ ○ ○ ○ ○
   ○ ○ ○ ○ ○
   ○ ○ ○ ○ ○

3. Add.

   A. $3 + 5 =$ _____

   B. $30 + 50 =$ _____

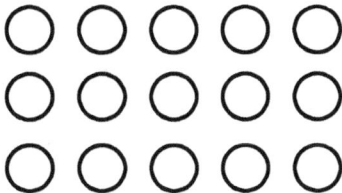

2. What are 2 related facts for $13 - 7 = 6$?

   ____ + ____ =

   ____ − ____ =

4. Colour $\frac{2}{3}$ of the shape.

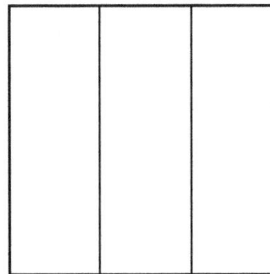

WEDNESDAY Geometry

1. Colour the shapes that are the same size and shape.

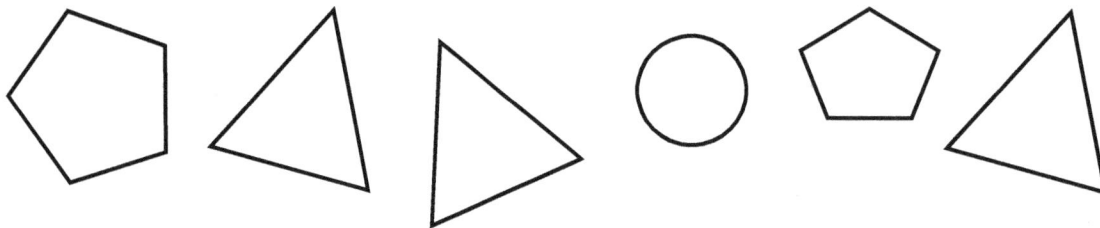

2. Look at the shapes. Choose flip, slide, or turn.

A. flip   B. slide   C. turn

3. How many sides does this shape have?

THURSDAY Measurement

1. What time will it be 1 hour later?

_____ : _____

2. Which set holds more?

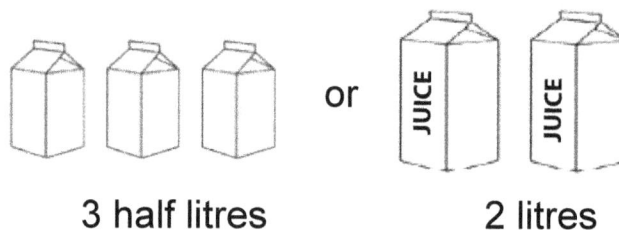

or

3 half litres   2 litres

3. If you have 4 dimes and 3 nickels, how many cents do you have? Use pictures and words.

_____ cents

4. Compare the lengths. Which length is longer than the line?

_____

A.

B.

Data Management

Here are the results of a Favourite Transportation survey.
Complete the tally chart and answer the questions.

Favourite Transportation

	Number	Tally
	9	
	17	
	13	

1. Circle the most popular mode of transportation.

2. Circle the least popular mode of transportation.

3. How many people liked [bicycle] more than [skateboard] ? _____

BRAIN STRETCH

Bill wants to buy a fishing rod for $1.00. He has 90¢.
How much more money does Bill need to buy the fishing rod?

MONDAY — Patterning and Algebra

1. What is the missing number to make the equation true?

   $6 + 4 + 7 = 2 +$ _____

2. What is the next number if the pattern rule is subtract 2?

   22, _____

3. There are 9 cupcakes on a plate. Maria and her friends ate 4 cupcakes. Then her mom put 7 more cupcakes on the plate. How many cupcakes are there now? Use pictures and an equation to show your work.

   _____

   ____ cupcakes

TUESDAY — Number Sense and Operations

1. Find the sum. Write the equation.

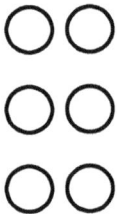

   ◯ ◯
   ◯ ◯
   ◯ ◯

   _____

2. Write the number.

   A. seventeen _____

   B. thirteen _____

   C. zero _____

3. Add.

   $20 + 46 =$ _____

4. Draw 4 coins to make 40 cents.

WEDNESDAY Geometry

1. Colour the shapes that are the same size and shape.

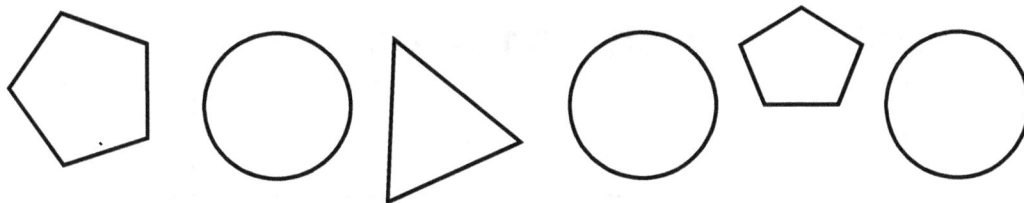

2. Look at the shapes.
   Choose flip, slide, or turn.

   A. flip   B. slide   C. turn

3. How many vertices does this shape have?

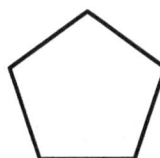

THURSDAY Measurement

1. Write the time in two ways.

   _____ : _____

   quarter to _____

2. Draw a line 3 centimetres long.

3. What is the **perimeter**?

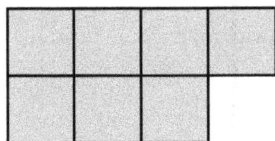

   _____ units

4. What is the **area**?

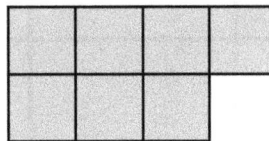

   _____ square units

FRIDAY Data Management

Ben went fishing. Look at the chart to see the number of fish Ben caught from Monday to Friday.

Number of Fish Ben Caught

Day of the Week	Monday	Tuesday	Wednesday	Thursday	Friday
Number of Fish Caught	2	4	6	8	10

1. On what day did Ben catch the most number of fish? _____

2. On what day did Ben catch the least number of fish? _____

3. What is the difference between the most number of fish Ben caught and the least number of fish? _____

BRAIN STRETCH

Complete the chart. Show three different ways to make $1.00 with coins.

Ways to Make $1.00 Using Coins

$1.00				
$1.00				
$1.00				

Week 30

Math — Show What You Know!

_____

☐ I read the question and I know what I need to find.

☐ I drew a picture or a diagram to help solve the question.

☐ I showed all the steps in solving the question.

☐ I used math language to explain my thinking.

Student Tracking Sheet

Student	Week 1	Week 2	Week 3	Week 4	Week 5	Week 6	Week 7	Week 8	Week 9	Week 10	Week 11	Week 12	Week 13	Week 14	Week 15

Student Tracking Sheet

Student	Week 16	Week 17	Week 18	Week 19	Week 20	Week 21	Week 22	Week 23	Week 24	Week 25	Week 26	Week 27	Week 28	Week 29	Week 30

You Are Incredible!

Keep Up the Good Work!

_____

Week 1, pages 1–3

Monday   **1.** Accept any repeating pattern with a matching explanation.   **2.** 4   **3.** 22, 24, 26

Tuesday   **1.** 6 tens, 5 ones, number 65   **2.** 16   **3.** 10; 11   **4.** A

Wednesday   **1.** triangle   **2.** 3   **3.** 3

Thursday   **1.** 7:00   **2.** cold   **3.** A   **4.** 3

Friday   **1.** 5   **2.** 4   **3.**   **4.**

Brain Stretch   9 balloons

Week 2, pages 4–6

Monday   **1.** Accept any repeating pattern.   **2.** 6   **3.** 80, 90, 100

Tuesday   **1.** 4 tens, 8 ones, number 48   **2. A.** 10 **B.** 13   **3.** 8; 9   **4.** C

Wednesday   **1.** circle   **2.** 0   **3.** 0

Thursday   **1.** B   **2.** B   **3.** A   **4.** 1

Friday   **1.** 8   **2.** 5   **3.** 3   **4.** 16

Brain Stretch   6 ants

Week 3, pages 7–9

Monday   **1.** Accept any repeating pattern with a matching rule.   **2.** Sample answer: 6 + 4 = 10; 10 + 8 = 18

Tuesday   **1.** 5 tens, 1 ones, number 51   **2. A.** 7 tens, 4 ones

B. 8 tens, 2 ones   **3.**   **4.** B

Wednesday   **1.** square   **2.** 4   **3.** 4

Thursday   **1.** 6:00   **2.** A   **3.** B   **4.** 4

Friday   **1.** 16   **2.** circle   **3.** square   **4.** triangle, rectangle

Brain Stretch   9 pieces of bubble gum

Week 4, pages 10–12

Monday   **1.** The coloured numbers line up vertically and skip a column, in an AB pattern.   **2.** 70

Tuesday   **1.** 4 tens, 0 ones, number 40   **2. A.** > **B.** =   **3.**   **4.** B

Wednesday   **1.** rectangle   **2.** 4   **3.** 4

Thursday   **1.** 1:30   **2.** B   **3.** A   **4.** 7

Friday   **1.** 8   **2.** 3   **3.** 7   **4.** 18

Brain Stretch   32 stamps

Week 5, pages 13–15

Monday   **1.** The coloured numbers line up vertically and end in 5 or 0.   **2.** 85

Tuesday   **1.** 4 tens, 3 ones, number 43   **2.**   **3.** 20, 46, 74   **4. A.** 15 **B.** 10

Wednesday   **1.** pentagon   **2.** 5   **3.** 5

Thursday   **1.** 8:30   **2.** December   **3.** C   **4.** 2

Friday   **1.** 8   **2.** 16   **3.** 10   **4.** 6

Brain Stretch   7 apples

Week 6, pages 16–18

Monday   **1.** The numbers line up vertically in a single row and all end in 0.   **2.** 70

Tuesday   **1.** 7 tens, 3 ones, number 73   **2. A.** 18 **B.** 16   **3. A.** 5 tens, 7 ones **B.** 8 tens, 2 ones   **4.** B

Wednesday   **1.** hexagon   **2.** 6   **3.** 6

Thursday   **1.** A   **2.** A   **3.** B   **4.** 5

Friday   The Favourite Zoo Animal Graph should extend shading to: 6 for Lion, 2 for Zebra, 5 for Flamingo, and 3 for Giraffe   **1.** 16   **2.** lion   **3.** zebra   **4.** 8

Brain Stretch   7 stamps

Week 7, pages 19–21

Monday   **1. 1.** 12, 15, 18   **2.** 13   **3.** 13   **4.** striped, solid, empty; ABC

Tuesday   **1.** 8 tens, 5 ones, number 85   **2.** ≠   **3.** 8 + 8 = 16, subtract 1 = 15, so 8 + 7 = 15   **4.** 35¢

Wednesday   **1.** octagon   **2.** 8   **3.** 8

Thursday   **1.** The long hand should point to 12 and the short hand to 5.   **2.** 2 hours
   3. Line should be 2 cm long.   **4.** Line is approximately 2 shoes long.

Friday   **1.** 7   **2.** 4   **3.** 6   **4.** 17   **5.** oranges

Brain Stretch   **1.** 15   **2.** 13   **3.** 9   **4.** 9 + 5 + 3 = 17; 17 pens

Week 8, pages 22–24

Monday   **1.** 105, 110, 115, 120   **2.** 7   **3.** ○△○; AB

Tuesday   **1.** 6 tens, 4 ones, number 64   **2.** ≠   **3. A.** 80 **B.** 35   **4.** 20¢

Wednesday   **1.** parallelogram   **2.** 4   **3.** 4

Thursday   **1.** 12:30   **2.** 4 hours   **3.** A   **4.** Lines should measure 3 cm.

Friday   The Favourite Pets Chart tally column: Dog 卌 ||||; Cat 卌 ||; Hamster ||||; Bird ||
   The Favourite Pets Graph should extend shading to 9 for dog, 7 for cat, 4 for hamster, and 2 for bird.
   1. dog   **2.** bird   **3.** 11   **4.** 3

Brain Stretch   **1.** 13   **2.** 20   **3.** 6   **4.** 9

Week 9, pages 25–27

Monday   **1.** 65   **2.** 8 + 5 = 13. So 13 − 8 = 5.   **3.** □■; AB

Tuesday   **1.** 4 tens, 5 ones, number 45   **2.** <   **3.** 9 + 9 = 18, subtract 1 = 17, so 9 + 8 = 17   **4.** 40¢

Wednesday   **1.** trapezoid   **2.** 4   **3.** 4

Thursday   **1.** 2:25   **2.** A   **3.** Friday   **4.** B

Friday   The Favourite Cookie Chart Tally Column: Chocolate Chip 卌 卌 ||; Oatmeal Raisin 卌 |||; Gingerbread ||||
   1. 12   **2.** 8   **3.** 8   **4.** chocolate chip

Brain Stretch   **1.** 25   **2.** 36 − 2 = 34   **3.** 40 + 3 = 43   **4.** 28 − 2 = 26

Week 10, pages 28–30

Monday   **1.** 52, add ten   **2.** 6   **3.** Sample patterns where only size of shape changes.

Tuesday   **1.** 5 tens, 3 ones, number 53   **2.** 2 + 8 = 10, 10 − 2 = 8 or 10 − 8 = 2
   3. A. 80 + 4 **B.** 20 + 9   **4.** 45¢

Wednesday   **1.** cylinder   **2.** 2   **3.** 3   **4.** C

Thursday   **1.** 4:40   **2.** 10:30   **3.** 12 months   **4.** B

Friday   The Favourite Shape Graph should extend shading to 4 for Hexagon, 3 for Heart, and 7 for Circle.
   1. circle   **2.** heart   **3.** 14   **4.** 4

Brain Stretch   **1.** 17   **2.** 14   **3.** 27   **4.** 35

Week 11, pages 31–33

Monday   **1.** 6   **2.** 9   **3.** ▽◯▽ ; ABB

Tuesday   **1.** 3 tens, 2 ones, number 32   **2.** No; even

3. Three of the four parts should be coloured.   **4.** 45¢

Wednesday   **1.** cube   **2.** 12   **3.** 6   **4.** ◯   **5.** A

Thursday   **1.** half past 2   **2.** A   **3.** B   **4.** A

Friday   **1.** broccoli   **2.** 5   **3.** carrots   **4.** 11

Brain Stretch   **1.** 89   **2.** 51   **3.** 30   **4.** 32

Week 12, pages 34–36

Monday   **1.** 3   **2.** 7 − 4 + 8 = 11; 11   **3.** 130, 140, 150, 160   **4.** 0

Tuesday   **1.** 9 tens, 6 ones, number 96   **2.** >   **3. A.** 17 **B.** 9   **4.** 80¢

Wednesday   **1.** cone   **2.** 1   **3.** 2   **4.** Sample answer: △   **5.** A

Thursday   **1.** 8:15, quarter past 8   **2.** A   **3.** C   **4.** 2

Friday   **1.** 30   **2.** Monday   **3.** 5   **4.** Friday

Brain Stretch   **1.** 58   **2.** 107   **3.** 31   **4.** 63

Week 13, pages 37–39

Monday   **1.** 1   **2.** 3 + 3 + 3 + 3 = 12   **3.** Accept any pattern with a matching rule.

Tuesday   **1.** 6 tens, 6 ones, number 66   **2.** 5 of 6 boxes should be coloured.

3. A. 19 **B.** 11   **4.** 45¢

Wednesday   **1.** rectangular prism   **2.** 12   **3.** 6   **4.** ☐   **5.** A

Thursday   **1.** 4:15, quarter past 4   **2.** B   **3.** A   **4.** A

Friday   Bar graphs should be shaded to 5 for spring, 10 for summer, 2 for autumn, and 9 for winter.

1. 15   **2.** 4   **3.** autumn   **4.** 19

Brain Stretch   **1.** 59   **2.** 80   **3.** 61   **4.** 40

Week 14, pages 40–42

Monday   **1.** +   **2.** 16   **3.** circle, heart, circle, heart   **4.** 90, 92, 94, 96

Tuesday   **1.** llllll ●●●   **2.** odd; There is one circle left over so 5 is odd.

3. 2 of 4 parts should be shaded.   **4.** 60¢

Wednesday   **1.** sphere   **2.** 0   **3.** 1   **4.** ☐   **5.** A

Thursday   **1.** 12:15, quarter past 12   **2.** 14 days   **3.** 52 weeks   **4.** 14

Friday   Favourite Breakfast Food chart Tally column: Cereal ⱵⱵ; Eggs ⱵⱵ ⱵⱵ; Pancakes ⱵⱵ l; Granola ⱵⱵ l

1. eggs   **2.** 11   **3.** pancakes and granola   **4.** cereal

Brain Stretch   **1.** 89   **2.** 79   **3.** 71   **4.** 51

Week 15, pages 43–45

Monday   **1.** ≠   **2.** 8   **3.** 5

Tuesday   **1.** llllll ●●●●●●●●   **2. A.** 7 **B.** 30   **3. A.** even **B.** odd   **4.** 60¢

Wednesday   **1.** pyramid   **2.** 8   **3.** 5   **4.** ⬠   **5.** B

Thursday   **1.** B   **2.** February   **3.** 365 days   **4.** Lines should measure 5 cm.

Friday   **1.** juice   **2.** water   **3.** 36   **4.** lemonade and milk

Brain Stretch   51; 51

Week 16, pages 46–48

Monday	**1.** ≠	**2.** 7	**3.** 4	**4.** 3 + 3 + 3 + 3 + 3 = 15

Tuesday   **1.** 4 tens, 2 ones, number 42   **2.** 73 > 21 > 17   **3.** 3 + 5 = 8, 8 – 3 = 5 or 8 – 5 = 3
4. One side of the shape should be coloured.

Wednesday   **1.** The 3 triangles should be coloured.   **2.** ◯   **3.** A

Thursday   **1.** 6:15, quarter past 6   **2.** A   **3.** A   **4.** 9

Friday   **1.** Those on the left side: Ben, Alma, Tiffany, Victoria   **2.** Those on the right side: Sylvia, Paula, Arthur, Juan, Cory, Maria   **3.** Those in the middle: Katie and Mike

Brain Stretch   **1.** 84   **2.** 90   **3.** 26   **4.** 16

Week 17, pages 49–51

Monday   **1.** =   **2.** 7   **3.** 2   **4.** 25

Tuesday   **1.** IIIIIIIII ● ● ● ●   **2.** 5 + 7 = 12, 12 – 7 = 5 or 12 – 5 = 7
3. A. 12 **B.** 41   **4.** One section of the shape should be coloured.

Wednesday   **1.** The first, third, and fifth pentagons should be coloured.   **2.** ◯   **3.** B

Thursday   **1.** 3:45, quarter to 4   **2.** B   **3.** A   **4.** 13

Friday   **1.** Those on the far left: Jessie, Avita, Carlos, Jeffery, Alice, Sandra   **2.** Those in the right circle: Linda, Leah, Amanda, Dana, James, John   **3.** Those on the far right: Leah, Amanda, Dana, James, John

Brain Stretch   **1.** 95   **2.** 75   **3.** 28   **4.** 29

Week 18, pages 52–54

Monday   **1.** =   **2.** repeating   **3.** Accept any number pattern with matching rule.   **4.** 42, 41, 40

Tuesday   **1. A.** 70 **B.** 300   **2.** Fewest coins to 75: 3 quarters   **3.** 6 tens, 3 ones   **4.** One hippopotamus should be circled.

Wednesday   **1.** Colours, in order: red, yellow, blue, green   **2.** A   **3.** A

Thursday   **1.** The short hand should point to 11 and the long hand to 9.   **2.** 4; 4 cm   **3.** B   **4.** 10

Friday   **1.** Those on the far left: Jacob, Isabella, Noah   **2.** Those on the far right: William, Jimmy, Grace   **3.** 3

Brain Stretch   **1.** 90   **2.** 87   **3.** 24   **4.** 36

Week 19, pages 55–57

Monday   **1.** 20   **2.** 25   **3.** growing   **4.** 32

Tuesday   **1. A.** 8 **B.** 9   **2.** 9 + 7 = 16 or 7 + 9 = 16, 16 – 9 = 7   **3. A.** 30 + 8 **B.** 20 + 9
4. One side of the shape should be coloured.

Wednesday   **1.** Colours, in order: orange, blue, red, and green   **2.** A   **3.** Sample answer: ▢

Thursday   **1.** 9:15, quarter past 9   **2.** B   **3.** Line should be 9 cm long.   **4.** May

Friday   **1.** Those on the far left: Sophie, Chris, Gina   **2.** 6   **3.** Those in the middle: David, Demetra, Andrew

Brain Stretch   36 – 17 = 19; 19

Week 20, pages 58–60

Monday   **1.** 10   **2.** 30   **3.** shrinking   **4.** Accept any repeating pattern where only colour changes.

Tuesday   **1.** C   **2.** 8 + 5 = 13 or 5 + 8 = 13, 13 – 8 = 5   **3. A.** odd **B.** odd
4. One section of the shape should be coloured.

Wednesday   **1.** Colours, in order: green, blue, red, orange   **2.** B   **3.** △

Thursday   **1.** 5:15, quarter past 5   **2.** November   **3.** B   **4.** 44 – 18 = 26; 26 centimetres taller

Friday   **1.** 31   **2.** Saturday   **3.** Monday   **4.** Thursday

Brain Stretch   Accept any 3 irregular shapes with 4 sides

Week 21, pages 61–63

Monday   **1.** 11   **2.** 9 + 11 = 20; 20   **3.** Accept any pattern with a matching rule.

Tuesday   **1.** B   **2.** B   **3.** 3 quarters, 1 dime, 1 nickel   **4.** One penguin should be circled.

Wednesday   **1.** The right 3 shapes should be coloured: hexagon, square, pentagon   **2.** B   **3.** Sample answer:

Thursday   **1.** 10:45, quarter to 11   **2.** 3 hours   **3.** A   **4.** A. calendar

Friday   **1.** 30   **2.** Friday   **3.** Tuesday   **4.** Saturday

Brain Stretch   14 pets

Week 22, pages 64–66

Monday   **1.** 3   **2.** 15   **3.** Accept any alternating pattern.

Tuesday   **1.** A   **2.** 2 of 6 squares should be shaded.   **3.** 67   **4.** One turtle should be circled.

Wednesday   **1.** The hexagon and octagon should be coloured.   **2.** A

           3. Accept any line that creates two equal halves.

Thursday   **1.** 11:15, quarter past 11   **2.** 100 cm   **3.** 6 squares   **4.** 8 squares

Friday   **1.** favourite meals   **2.** dinner   **3.** lunch   **4.** dinner

Brain Stretch   18 frogs

Week 23, pages 67–69

Monday   **1.** ≠   **2.** 11   **3.** Accept any pattern with a matching rule.

Tuesday   **1.** B   **2.** Yes. 40 + 20 = 60; 5 + 5 = 10; 60 + 10 = 70; So, 45 + 25 = 70.   **3. A.** 50 **B.** 70

           4. 5 + 8 = 13, 13 − 5 = 8 or 13 − 8 = 5

Wednesday   **1.** All shapes but the triangle should be coloured.   **2.** B   **3.**

Thursday   **1.** 8:45, quarter to 9   **2.** B   **3.** 6 squares   **4.** 9 squares

Friday   **1.** apples   **2.** grapes   **3.** grapes < bananas < apples   **4.** 11   **5.** 6

Brain Stretch   92 jelly beans

Week 24, pages 70–72

Monday   **1.** 31   **2.** 3 + 12 + 4 = 19; 19   **3.** 59   **4.** Accept any pattern with a matching rule.

Tuesday   **1.** C   **2.** 3 of 5 parts should be shaded.   **3. A.** 7 **B.** 4 **C.** 11   **4.**

Wednesday   **1.** All but the octagon and the hexagon should be coloured.   **2.** A   **3.** B

Thursday   **1.** 10:00   **2.** Accept a line 5 cm long.   **3.** 4; 4; fourth   **4.** 12 squares

Friday   **1.** pop   **2.** country   **3.** pop > rock > country   **4.** 22   **5.** 12

Brain Stretch   48 hockey cards

Week 25, pages 73–75

Monday   **1.** 42   **2.** 76   **3.** 560, 570, 580, 590, 600   **4.** Accept a pattern where shape changes.

Tuesday   **1.** 34   **2.** 90, 85, 76   **3. A.** 50 **B.** 90   **4.**

Wednesday   **1.** In order, the objects should be coloured: blue, yellow, green, red, yellow, blue, red   **2.** A   **3.**

Thursday   **1.** The short hand should point between 10 and 11, and the long hand should point to the 5.   **2.** B

           3. 15 squares   **4.** 2; half

Friday   The bar graph should be shaded to 6 for Art, 9 for Language, 8 for Math, 8 for Science, and 4 for Music.

           1. language   **2.** 14   **3.** Math and science.

Brain Stretch   60 cookies

Week 26, pages 76–78

Monday **1.** 160, 170, 180, 190 **2.** 26 **3.** 17 − 9 = 8; 8

Tuesday **1.** 149 **2.** 2 + 2 + 2 + 2 + 2 + 2 = 12 **3. A.** 10 **B.** 20 **4.** [row of animal icons with the 6th circled]

Wednesday **1.** C **2.** A **3.** B **4.** Sample answer: H

Thursday **1.** 2:45, quarter to 3 **2.** B **3.** B **4.** 8

Friday **1.** Ferris wheel **2.** The roller coaster and the merry-go-round. **3.** 4 **4.** 8

Brain Stretch 24 ants

Week 27, pages 79–81

Monday **1.** 190, 195, 200, 205 **2.** 52 **3.** Accept pattern where size changes **4.** ≠

Tuesday **1.** 3 quarters and 1 nickel **2.** B **3. A.** 4 **B.** 40 **4.** 9 + 5 = 14 or 5 + 9 = 14, 14 − 9 = 5

Wednesday **1.** Colour of shapes, in order: blue, red, blue, yellow, green, red, yellow **2.** B **3.** B

Thursday **1.** The long hand ponts to the 9. **2.** July **3.** 5 cm line. **4.** 0°C

Friday The Favourite Colour numbers should be: 9 Red, 13 Blue, 8 Green, and 2 Yellow

1. blue **2.** yellow **3.** 10 **4.** blue > red > green > yellow

Brain Stretch 10 nickels

Week 28, pages 82–84

Monday **1.** 51 **2.** 68 **3.** Colour changing pattern **4.** 14

Tuesday **1.** 5 + 5 + 5 + 5 = 20 or 4 + 4 + 4 + 4 + 4 = 20 **2.** B **3.** 9 + 3 = 12, 12 − 9 = 3 or 12 − 3 = 9 **4.** Three sections of the shape should be coloured.

Wednesday **1.** Colours, in order: red, blue, green, orange, green, red, orange **2.** A or B **3.** A

Thursday **1.** 9:00 **2.** Accept any answer 25°C or higher. **3.** 95 cents **4.** A

Friday **1.** Those on the far right: Stephen, Monique, Chloe **2.** Those in the left circle: Chris, Bess, Ethan

3. Those in the middle: Bess, Ethan

Brain Stretch 12 cupcakes

Week 29, pages 85–87

Monday **1.** 30 **2.** 33 **3.** Accept any pattern with a matching rule. **4.** 23 + 14 = 37 or 37 − 14 = 23; 23

Tuesday **1.** 3 + 3 + 3 + 3 + 3 = 15 or 5 + 5 + 5 = 15 **2.** 7 + 6 = 13, 13 − 6 = 7 **3. A.** 8 **B.** 80

4. 2 of 3 parts should be shaded

Wednesday **1.** The 3 triangles should be coloured. **2.** C **3.** 4

Thursday **1.** 2:30 **2.** 2 litres **3.** 55 cents **4.** B

Friday Favourite Transportation chart Tally column: Skateboard ||||| ||||; Bike ||||| ||||| ||||| ||; Scooter ||||| ||||| |||

1. bike **2.** skateboard **3.** 8

Brain Stretch 10¢

Week 30, pages 88–90

Monday **1.** 15 **2.** 20 **3.** 9 − 4 + 7 = 12; 12 cupcakes

Tuesday **1.** 3 + 3 = 6 or 2 + 2 + 2 = 6 **2. A.** 17 **B.** 13 **C.** 0 **3.** 66 **4.** 4 dimes

Wednesday **1.** The 3 circles should be coloured. **2.** A or C **3.** 5

Thursday **1.** 11:45, quarter to 12 **2.** 3 cm line **3.** 12 units **4.** 7 square units

Friday **1.** Friday **2.** Monday **3.** 8

Brain Stretch Sample answer: one loonie, four quarters, ten dimes, twenty nickels